Self-Marketing Secrets

Self-Marketing Secrets

Winning by Making Your Name Known

Henry DeVries and Diane Gage

Pfeiffer
& COMPANY

Amsterdam • Johannesburg • Oxford
San Diego • Sydney • Toronto

Published by
Pfeiffer & Company
8517 Production Avenue
San Diego, CA 92121-2280

Interior Design: Kachina Press
Cover: John Odam Design Associates

Library of Congress Cataloging-in-Publication Data
DeVries, Henry, and Gage, Diane
Self marketing Secrets: Winning by making your name known
1. Advertising—Professional 2. Advertising. 3. Marketing
HF6161.P89Dd48 1991
658.8'02—dc20 91-2334

ISBN: 0-932238-65-3

Printed in the United States of America.
Printing 3 4 5 6 7 8 9 10

Dedication

We want to give special thanks to our spouses, Vikki and Gene, and our children, Kevin Gage and Karla, Jack, Devin, and Jordan DeVries, for having the right stuff to live with people who are compelled to write stuff.

Contents

Preface

An old adage says it's not what you know, it's who you know. We take a different view. It's not what you know, but who knows *you*. Making your name known is the key to achieving success and finding new clients.

While there are numerous good books on how to market a product, there are few on how an individual can earn visibility. Most focus on how to be your own publicist or how to produce marketing materials like flyers and brochures. *Self-Marketing Secrets* looks at a different set of questions.

- How do you become a quoted expert in your field?
- What does it take to be invited to join prestigious boards of directors?
- How can you position yourself as an opinion leader?
- What can you do to move in circles that will propel your business ahead?
- How can you win top awards in your profession?

Self-Marketing Secrets teaches business owners, their sales forces, and company managers how to make their names known. We address such topics as gaining exposure, positioning, and making important linkages to expand a career or an enterprise. This book gives specific how-tos for personal marketing from giving speeches to becoming a quoted authority or entering competitions for increased recognition.

Because *Self-Marketing Secrets* is personalized, it complements how-to books for marketing an entrepreneurial enterprise. It gives readers insights into positioning themselves in the marketplace. This book expands on basic networking techniques and gives fresh insights into gaining the professional recognition and prestige that ultimately lead to increased sales.

Chapter 1 defines "Self-marketing" and explains our basic philosophy. Targeting and positioning, the first two steps in the 15-Step Self-Marketing Formula, are covered in practical terms. We owe part of the inspiration for the 15-Step Self-Marketing Formula to the writings of Linda Taber, a senior vice president of Ketchum Public Relations. It was Linda who wrote in the *P.R. Reporter* newsletter, "It's no longer true that, if you do a good job, everyone will know. The John Wayne days of the strong, silent type are over."

A pair of two-man teams must also be credited as sources of inspiration. The first pair is Glen Broom, Ph.D., and David Dozier, Ph.D., professors of journalism. Broom and Dozier have served as mentors to us in the use of research and planning. The second pair is Al Reis and Jack Trout, the writers of *Positioning the Battle for Your Mind* and *Marketing Warfare*. Their agency, Trout & Reis, Inc., has created marketing campaigns for some of the nation's largest corporations, including Xerox, Monsanto, and Burger King. Their writings not only provided the theory of positioning, a key element in the 15-Step Self-Marketing Formula, but also demonstrated to us the power of using self-marketing to promote a professional services firm.

Chapters 2 through 13 explain the how-tos of making your name known. We do not limit ourselves to professional examples only. If another example was more intriguing, we used it instead. We owe a special debt of gratitude to seminar student Janice Alessandra, who told us we have a message that should be shared. We also were inspired by Tony Alessandra, Ph.D., a former college professor and a renowned sales trainer and self-marketing genius. Tony took the time to provide valuable insights before we even had a working concept.

Another man who invested time in this book was Lee Shapiro, a former lawyer and judge, who is now an outstanding motivational speaker. He introduced us to a world of expert self-marketers, whose successes helped shape the ideas in this book. Thanks also are owed Teresee Henney, who served as an unpaid researcher.

Chapter 14 is about planning. We know, we know. Planning should come first, not last. But before we could tell you how to pull this together in a plan, we want you to know what the possibilities are. Again, we owe thanks to Broom and Dozier for their teachings. Further planning inspiration came from the speeches and writings of Fred Pryor, who says, "Creativity is not reserved for the gifted," and Zig Ziglar, who says, "You can get whatever you want in life if you just help enough people get what they want." That has been our mission.

Write When You Find Work

A final thanks to all those people who contributed ideas and examples. We want even more. If you have good examples, or you wish to share how this book has helped you, please let us know. Maybe we can include them if we sell the book as a TV mini-series.

Please write to us at:

Henry DeVries and Diane Gage
c/o The Gage Group
8885 Rio San Diego Drive, Suite 335
San Diego, CA 92108

A Special Acknowledgment

We are deeply indebted to a special team that helped bring this book together. Susan "Noonie" Benford worked her red pen magic, and we are still congratulating ourselves that she agreed to be our editor. Robyn Bottomley was relentless, as always, on the phone and served admirably as researcher. Jennifer North was always gracious under pressure as our fact checker and typist. JoAnn Padgett gave the book a final edit and made us look smarter. Special thanks to you all. It is easy to be good coaches when you have superstars on your team.

1

How to Position Yourself
for Success
My Niche Is Better Than Your Niche

Sometimes a line in a motion picture says it all. For this book, the film is *The Natural.* Robert Redford stars as Roy Hobbs, a baseball player of rare ability whose life did not turn out as he expected. In an opening scene, it is a spring day in rural 1920s America. Roy is a school boy growing up on the family farm, and his dad is teaching him how to play baseball. His father realizes, during a game of catch by the barn, that Roy could be the greatest baseball star of all time. The father, who expects to die soon, wonders what to tell Roy to prepare him for the rough journey ahead. He gives him this fatherly advice: "You got a gift, Roy. But it's not enough. You got to develop yourself. Rely too much on your gift and you will fail."

Here is our pitch to you. If you have a service or skill to sell, being gifted is not enough. If you rely too much on being good at what you do, you will fail. Gaining recognition is the way to win new clients. It is essential to have an image and a reputation that attract referrals, recommendations, and results. *Self-Marketing Secrets* shows you how.

We are happy to confess that none of the strategies in this book is our own. As wise King Solomon said twenty-five centuries ago, there is nothing new under the sun. This is not the product of original thinking, it is something better. What we have done is study the strategies that savvy megabuck marketing departments use to position their corporations above the competition. We then took these proven ideas and gave them a new twist. We applied that research to the individual—be it a professional, an entrepreneur, or a small businessperson.

All ideas were then tested for more than five years. We used the self-marketing concepts to attract clients to our respective marketing consulting firms, and we used the strategies to win customers for our clients and students. We did this through the following: extensive consulting, teaching university extended studies courses, conducting seminars, and speaking to professional groups. Below is a list of some who have profited.

Accountants	Entrepreneurs
Agents	Financial Planners
Architects	Insurance Agents
Authors	Inventors
Bankers	Lawyers
Brokers	Photographers
Builders	Psychiatrists
Consultants	Psychologists
Contractors	Real Estate Agents
Dentists	Sales Consultants
Designers	Speakers
Doctors	Store Owners
Engineers	Tax Preparers

Over and over professionals tell us, "I'm good at what I do, but I don't know marketing. What can I do to win more new business?" We know it isn't easy, because we face the same challenges. How do you do good work for the clients you have and still find time to land more clients? Plus, after you pay the bills, there's no money left for marketing. But there is an answer. We will show you how with our 15-Step Self-Marketing Formula. Before we discuss the steps, we need to examine the philosophy behind *Self-Marketing Secrets.*

Debunking the Good Work Myth

A myth is a traditional story that concerns supernatural events. Almighty Zeus, rewarding good and punishing evil from his court on Mount Olympus, was one myth the ancient Greeks used to explain their world. Myths are different from legends, which are about human actions, and different from fairy tales, which are inventions to amuse or to teach. Myths explain what can't be explained.

For many professionals, what attracts clients can't be explained, which is understandable. Most are not formally educated in marketing. If they are, this type of marketing is rarely covered in college courses. Marketing a service is different from marketing a product. For one thing, profit margins are smaller and don't leave much room for marketing budgets. Even if there is money, typical advertising sends out the wrong messages. For many service firms, hard-sell advertising just doesn't look professional.

When coauthor Henry DeVries began to work for a public relations agency, he wondered why the firm was so successful. It was one of the largest independent public relations agencies in America. When Henry asked the president why they won so many new clients, he was told, "We do very good work. New business just keeps landing on our doorstep."

On the surface, this makes a lot of sense. Even the Bible's Book of Proverbs says, "Have you seen a man skillful in his work? Before kings is where he will station himself." But doing a great job will take you only so far. There is no reliable source of information about who is the best attorney, accountant, architect, and so on. The best are not always in demand. People don't clamor for their services.

Word-of-mouth advertising, which we are told is the best way to promote your business, is very logical. It explains things. But it's just not true. For years, Hershey's executives bragged that word-of-mouth was the only marketing they needed to sell chocolate bars, until they noticed how fast Hershey's was losing customers and market share. Neither great chocolate, nor great work alone, will do it. There is no Professional Services Zeus who sends new clients to the doorsteps of those who are good and thunderbolts to the behinds of those who aren't. Let's eliminate this myth once and for all.

The Good Work Myth
It Is A Myth That
If You Do Good Work,
New Business Will Land On Your Doorstep.

This myth assumes that quality of work is the only factor. Yes, you should work hard at being very good. You can't use our Self-Marketing Formula unless you are good. But how do people judge quality?

To Know Me Is to Like Me

Based on classic persuasion research (developed in Carl Hovland's Yale Communication Program) and practical studies (commissioned for Henry DeVries' clients), we believe that most people judge professionals based on whether they have heard of them or not. As long as what they have heard is positive or neutral, and not negative, then recognition is what counts.

Henry recently left consulting to work fulltime with an organization that has just such a problem. Their challenge illustrates the point we want to make. The group is a not-for-profit, fraternal benefit society called the Independent Order of Foresters (IOF), and some of the examples in this book are from this organization.

Interestingly, these Foresters have nothing to do with trees. The name originated in medieval England when a group of people who worked in the forest banded together to help each other's families.

Established in 1874, IOF is a membership organization that helps families. Only about five percent of the population has heard about it because the organization has never advertised or promoted itself. The group hosts social activities, participates in community projects, and helps members in time of need.

For a family, joining the IOF is a good deal. But, remember, being good isn't good enough. The IOF has more than 1 million members and $2 billion in assets but faces a major challenge in recruiting new members. When all of the benefits for a family are explained and the prospective members are told how little it costs to join, this is what they say: "This is too good to be true. If there was something this good out there, I would have heard about it." However, the more they have heard about it, the more willing they are to join. This is called the recognition factor.

The Recognition Factor
This Is How People Think:
If I Have Not Heard Of You,
You Can't Be Very Good.

Most businesses or consultants do gain a good share of their work through referrals. People recommend two types of professionals: those they have worked with, and those whose names they have heard a lot. The converse to the recognition factor is also true: If I have heard a lot about you, you must be good. Remember though, it has to be positive or at least neutral. If they have heard a lot about you because you were just indicted for tax evasion, that won't help you.

People Hire People, Not Firms

About three years after he joined a big public relations agency, Henry wanted to start a firm of his own. He worried about how he would get new business. Henry knew that there was more to it than just doing good work. He had an acute case of what teaching professionals call "a need to know." When your college professor recommended a book, you probably never read it. But when the professor said tomorrow's final exam would be based solely on that same book, suddenly you wanted to read it very badly. Or learning how to sky dive might not hold much appeal to you, unless you have a parachute and your plane just ran out of fuel. That's what is called a need to know.

So Henry carefully analyzed his employer. It was true the firm never promoted itself through advertising, direct mail, or cold sales calls. However, it consistently did other activities to attract clients.

- The president had risen to the top ranks of leadership in the local chamber of commerce.
- The senior vice president and partner was appointed to a high-ranking county commission.
- Both principals were quoted extensively in the media as industry experts.
- Both principals gave speeches to business groups.
- Winning awards was a high priority for the firm.

So doing good work was important, but equally important was being recognized as a leader in the profession. Henry then looked at other firms and other professions. What was different about this type of marketing over product marketing? Traditional marketing looks at the four *P's:* promotion, place, price, and product. One part of the company makes the product and the other part of the business sells the product. But what is the product of service marketing? It is people, namely the principals of the firm. A service firm is of the product, by the product, and for the product.

A quote from author and cartoonist James Thurber illustrates this point. A woman once approached Thurber at a party and asked how things were. "Things, madam, will take care of themselves. It's people who concern me." And it is the people who do the work that concern the prospects. It is the coauthors' opinion that, even if you have twenty people working for you, you have to sell yourself and not the firm. This is what *Self-Marketing Secrets* is all about.

The Self-Marketing Secret
People Hire People, Not Firms.
You Must Market Yourself As the Expert.

The 15-Step Self-Marketing Formula

This is not a theoretical book. If anything, we sacrifice explaining *why* self-marketing works in favor of giving you more examples of *how* it works. Perhaps when it comes to self-marketing we are like the subject of Isaac Asimov's joke about Pierre Simon Laplace, the great French mathematician and astronomer of Napoleon's day. In his book, *Isaac Asimov's Treasury of Humor,* Asimov describes what "obvious" means to a scientist like Laplace.

"A professor of physics, deriving some profound point of theory for the class, scribbled an equation on the board and said, 'From this, it is obvious that we can proceed to write the following relationship,' and he scribbled a second equation on the board.

"Then he paused. He stared hard at the two equations and said, 'Wait awhile. I may be wrong.'

"He sat down, seized a pad and started to write furiously. He paused for thought, crossed out what he had written, and began over. In this fashion, half an hour passed while the class held its breath and sat in absolute silence.

"Finally, the professor rose with an air of satisfaction and said, 'Yes, I was right in the first place. It *is* obvious that the second equation follows the first.'" (From *Treasury of Humor* by Isaac Asimov. Copyright© 1971 by Isaac Asimov. Reprinted by permission of Houghton Mifflin Co.)

Laplace often wrote in *Celestial Mechanics,* his five-volume book on how the universe functioned, a mathematical equation followed by the line, "From this it is easy to see," and then moved on to the next equation. But it was not all that easy for the readers to see.

We hope it will be obvious why the Self-Marketing Formula works. Diane used this formula to found her public relations firm, the Gage Group. In eight years the firm has grown from just Diane at her kitchen table to eight employees in a river-front office building. Instead of forming his own firm when he left the big public relations agency, Henry joined an advertising and public relations firm that specialized in handling home builders. His mission was to use the formula to diversify the firm. When he left six years later, he was executive vice president and the client list included Marriott, Sunkist, and the Super Bowl. He helped the agency grow from just over $4 million in billings and 10 employees to more than $10 million in billings and 30 employees.

For all fifteen points in the formula, the coauthors speak from experience. We have helped clients put these steps into action, and we have done them all ourselves. When we recommend that you get published, we know that you can because between us we have written seven books and hundreds of magazine articles. We have spoken before thousands at national conventions, extended studies courses, chamber of commerce seminars, and even the local Lions Club. We have worked our way into the boards of directors of important organizations. Yes, it is hard work. But it is worth it. And you can do it too.

The Self-Marketing Formula

1. Research a target market
2. Determine positioning

3. Maximize memberships
4. Win awards
5. Become a quoted media authority
6. Become friends with the media
7. Publicize your name
8. Get published
9. Speak before prospects
10. Do charitable work
11. Form bonds through letters
12. Utilize direct mail
13. Try gimmicks
14. Use guerrilla advertising when necessary
15. Have a plan

Target Marketing When You're Low on Ammunition

Target marketing, where self-marketing really begins, means research. And research means doing your homework. You need to determine your Who, What and How: exactly Who your clients are going to be, What you will offer that will interest them, and How you will reach them.

Harvey Mackay, in *Swim with the Sharks without Being Eaten Alive*, says the Japanese have a simple way of describing the typical American marketing plan. "Ready? Fire! Aim!" We just go out and do it, then we try to figure out what went wrong. First we develop the product or service, then we try to figure out who needs it. Or maybe we try to create a need for it.

Most target marketing books and articles will tell you to research what the clients want, then tailor your service to meet those needs. For self-marketing, we say you must go even farther. You need to make yourself an expert on the subject; this research opens the door for all of the self-marketing avenues.

Here is a case in point. Sales trainer Tony Alessandra says that "most people aim at nothing and hit it with amazing accuracy." When he was a university professor, he decided to go into the sales training business. Although he had been very successful selling products door to door, Alessandra had never taken a course in sales. But he did know how to do research.

From reading and talking to salespeople, Alessandra determined that there was a need for an "honest approach to selling." This was the basis for his courses and subsequent book, *Non-Manipulative Selling.* He did not limit his research to what others had written about sales training. He went far afield to other disciplines like psychology. He found that most of the current sales training information was based on behavioral psychology of people like Pavlov and B. F. Skinner, which uses psychology against the buyer. Alessandra advocated a more humanistic approach based on the teachings of such people as Carl Rogers, which suggests working with the buyer.

Today Alessandra is not only an expert sales trainer, commanding fees of several thousand dollars for a one-hour talk, he also is an expert on how to develop a celebrity profile. He has spoken at various meetings of the National Speakers Association on the topic of how to use writing, speaking, and serving as a media expert to promote yourself.

Research Gives You the Edge

Starring in the film *When Harry Met Sally*, Meg Ryan plays a woman who never orders anything the way it appears on a restaurant menu. Waiters are given detailed lectures on how to prepare and arrange the food on the plate. Billy Crystal, as Harry, questions his date on why it takes her longer to order a meal than it does to eat it. Sally explains, "I want it the way I want it."

That says it all for target marketing research. Find out who your clients should be, and find out how they want it. This is called nichemanship. Look at things like

age
sex
race
occupation
education
income
activities
interests

beliefs
frequency of use of your service

Then watch for trends that concern your niche of the market by being an avid consumer of information. Segment one particular specialty and call it your own. Promote yourself as the specialist, the expert, the authority. Today's consumers demand more and more choices. Look back seventy-five years ago and this just wasn't so. Henry Ford was a pioneer automaker. His assembly line production set the market standard for efficiency. But he did nothing for market research. "You can have a Model T in any color you want," he used to say. "As long as it's black."

The term market research scares a lot of professionals. One objection is that they can't afford it. A second objection is that even if it is affordable, you can never really know what people want.

Let's dismiss the second objection first. Some question the reliability of surveys. How can we base decisions on what a few hundred randomly selected people say? For a discussion of how sampling works, we refer you to Glen Broom and Dave Dozier's book *Using Research in Public Relations*. But in short, for people who challenge sampling, we suggest that the next time they go in for a blood test they demand that the doctor remove all of their blood.

Others object that research cannot tell everything. This is true. At best, research is a dim nightlight that helps us grope our way through the dark. It is like the true story about the champion blind golfer who is willing to bet money he can beat any pro golfer on the men's tour. He just wants to know what day at midnight they want to tee off. A lot of professionals approach marketing like golfing in the dark. Wouldn't it be to your advantage if you could see better than the competition?

The first objection about price is easy to overcome. We live in an information age. Investing time in a trip to a good university library can give you more information than you will ever need. Read everything you can on your subject and then analyze your findings, in writing, in what market researchers call an analysis of secondary research. In high school you called it a term paper.

Let's say your target market is families and your profession is the law. First, what do families want today? A review of the *Reader's Guide to Periodical Literature* reveals forty-six articles in the last five years. Some of these include

- "Parenthood: A Special Report on Families Today" *Ladies Home Journal,* June 1990
- "The Future of the Family (Results of a Survey)," *Parents,* January 1990
- "This Is What You Thought: 93% Say Strong Family Ties Bring Happiness," *Glamour,* Febuary 1989
- "Children of the Future (Attitudes of Baby Boomers)," *Rolling Stone,* May 5, 1988

Next comes a review of books written on the subject. You need to go to two places: a university library and a well-stocked bookstore. On the subject of family, for instance, a University of California library lists 1,108 books with the word "family" in the title. Most are at least five years old. For newer material, a trip to the bookstore is in order.

The third thing to continually research is the law and how it impacts families. We live in a rapidly changing world. New legislation, court decisions, and government policy can have profound effects. You need to be a consumer educator on what families need to know about the law. Your industry's trade journals have everything you need.

Finding the information is not the challenge. In fact we heard it said that the experience is more like trying to get a sip of water from an open fire hydrant. The hard part is making sense of it. You must do the tough job of analyzing the information and putting it in terms people can easily understand.

Positioning in the Prospect's Mind

If you haven't already, read *Positioning: The Battle for Your Mind* and *Marketing Warfare* by Al Ries and Jack Trout. For a good summation of positioning, we refer you to the classic text *Contemporary Advertising* by Courtland Bovée and William Arens. Positioning has become a buzzword in marketing and advertising circles. The authors demonstrate the concept by asking a few simple questions. Who was the first person to fly solo across the Atlantic? Charles Lindbergh, of course. But who was the second? Not so easy. Who was the first person to walk on the moon? Neil Armstrong made that one small step for man, one giant leap for mankind. But who was the second man to walk on the moon? The first person to occupy a position in the prospect's mind is going to be hard to dislodge.

Ries and Trout compare the mind to a memory bank, with slots and positions for every bit of information to retain. But unlike a computer, which has to retain information fed to it, the mind does not. As a defense mechanism, the mind screens and rejects the flood of information. The mind keeps what agrees with its prior experience and filters out the rest.

To store the information, the mind ranks products and brands. Visualize a series of ladders. Say computers, and people think of IBM on the top rung. For electronics, it's Sony; for automobiles, it's Mercedes.

For self-marketing, it is critical that you earn enough recognition to make it onto the ladder for your category. The mind does not have room for things new and different, so you must relate them to the old. This is where nichemanship comes in. As an architect, you will be put on the architectural ladder. Frank Lloyd Wright is probably on the top rung. But you can be known as the architect who specializes in designing 1990s versions of Victorian homes.

Let's take law as an example. For years the top rung probably belonged to Melvin Belli, the attorney known as the "King of Torts." In her book *Expose Yourself*, former journalist turned public relations consultant Melba Beals describes how she helped create this positioning. But there is lots of room on the ladder. Describing yourself as the Melvin Belli of sexual harassment cases is not a bad strategy.

A good example of this is Dr. Joyce Rebhun, a former IRS tax attorney who calls herself a tax therapist. "I knew from studying marketing in college you have to differentiate yourself," says Rebhun. "There is already a glut on the market of tax attorneys."

Rebhun decided her target market would be those who have emergency tax problems with the IRS. Because she only handles crisis cases, she has been featured in numerous newspapers and magazine articles, as well as on TV news shows. She runs ads in newspapers with her photo and headlines that read "You Don't Need to Lose Your Job—Family—Sanity Because of the IRS." Her phone number is 1-800-SOS-4TAX. She may be on the crowded lawyer ladder, but she definitely has clearly defined her own rung. Even in her promotion, she never forgets positioning. She is starting a syndicated newspaper column called "Ask Dr. Joyce," which she describes as the "Dear Abby of the tax world."

Positioning Strategies to Consider

Each positioning strategy must be special. This will be the mental hook your prospective clients and the media use to attach you to the ladder in their minds. Here are several strategies to consider as you do your homework.

- Service expert—the Nordstrom of...
- High-quality expert—the Rolls Royce of...
- Low-price expert—the Rent-a-Wreck of...
- Fitness expert—the Jane Fonda of...
- Educated expert—the Harvard of...
- Low-calorie expert—the Lean Cuisine of...

You also can position by single or combined demographic group. You can be the women's expert, the senior citizen expert, the Asian expert, or even the Asian women's senior citizen expert. Geographic considerations like the Gulf Coast expert or Seattle expert, or industry considerations like the hotel expert or auto-wrecking yard expert should also be considered in your positioning.

An important final point—a positioning statement has to be brief. "Light, tight, and bright" is how one magazine editor describes it. Your positioning statement will not define the total you. We are all complex creatures, and volumes would not do us justice. Don't worry, you can and probably will need to handle other types of business and clients.

However, the positioning is the slot that will get your name remembered in the prospect's mind.

Top Self-Marketing Secrets
How to Position Yourself for Success

1. Don't believe the myth that if you do good work, new business will land on your doorstep.

2. People only believe you are good if they have heard of you.

3. People hire people, so you must market yourself.

4. Do your homework to find out who you should market to and what they want from your profession.

5. Determine a positioning strategy that will differentiate you from everyone else in your service category.

2

Don't Join Any Club That Would Have You As a Member
Seven Principles for Maximizing Membership Opportunities

How much do you expect to get from the membership dues you pay to join a business club? One man got $200,000 and enough linkages to launch a business. He was seeking capital and a seasoned manager to propel his two-year-old company into production. He found both the money and the man he was looking for at a local venture capital club, a new breed of organization evolving throughout the country during the past few years. Not only do the clubs welcome venture capitalists and entrepreneurs, but also investors, corporate managers looking for entrepreneurial jobs, and service providers such as attorneys, business plan consultants, and accountants seeking to expand their client base. In fact, an attorney garnered more than twenty clients through contacts he has made at venture capital club meetings.

It pays to be a joiner. To advance your career or build clientele, it's essential to take part in professional groups. Work toward becoming a leader of one or more clubs; do that by joining the right committee. Do some homework before volunteering. Determine the chairpersons and members of various committees, then join those comprised of people with whom you want to form linkages. Committees give you a chance to show your stuff (not just swap business cards), plus an opportunity to get to know all of the members. Use your status as a group member to seek advice from key players inside and outside the organization. Here are some recommendations to accomplish all that and more.

Principle One: Aspire Higher When Joining Up

Try to join groups in which you are one of the few representatives from your profession or corporate rank, rather than organizations comprised solely of professional colleagues.

It was Groucho Marx who sent the telegram, "Please accept my resignation. I don't want to belong to any club that would accept me as a member." We don't recommend being that snobbish, but it pays to aim above your station in selecting groups to join. If you know almost everyone in a group, or everyone flocks to meet you like a hungry car salesman when you arrive, it is time to investigate other groups.

If you are a female marketing professional who represents health care firms, it might be wise to join a group of health care communicators. But your time might be even better invested by joining women in health care administration so that you can get to know, on a personal level, the decision makers. You'll learn the hot spots within their organizations that affect whether or not there is the need or the budget to contract for outside marketing.

And when you find a group to join outside your profession, don't always sit on committees made up of others in your field. As a financial expert, you won't meet many you can market your services to if you volunteer for the finance committee—comprised of all the other financial bigwigs in town. Instead, why not join planning or program development and meet others who may some day want to hire you?

Principle Two: Let Someone Convince You to Join

Personal contacts made through these groups prove to be invaluable assets to both your career and your company or cause. So before you sign up, put on your Sherlock Holmes hat and do some sleuthing.

Set up an informational interview with the head of the organization or the membership committee chair to see how you will best fit in. Ask colleagues and industry leaders for their opinions of the group.

When one public relations professional wanted to move in new circles, she knew she should become involved in the chamber of commerce. Rather than joining the obvious—the marketing committee—she set up an informational interview with one of the chamber's vice presidents. During their forty-five minutes, she explained her goals to more aggressively position herself and her company and to learn more about her city and its business community.

The time they spent together gave the vice president a chance to get to know the potential volunteer on a personal level. A week later she called back and asked her to serve on a new committee that would provide a grant to an up-and-coming woman-owned business. Serving on the committee were extremely well-known women in the community—just the type of leaders the public relations professional wanted to meet.

When you are checking out a group, some key points to determine are

size of membership
image within the community or industry
"known activists" within the organization in leadership positions
your ability to obtain high visibility

If the group appears worth your time and energy, proceed to the second step. Attend a meeting and approach one of the group's friendlier leaders. Tell the leader you are impressed by the good things you have heard about the group. Then ask if it is a good group to join. *Let the leader sell you on joining the group.* When you join, tell the membership people that this leader convinced you to join. This serves two purposes. It allows you to break the ice with a key leader. Then when you join, the leader feels responsibility toward you. After all, it was thanks to the leader that you joined the club.

Principle Three: Mingle, Mingle, Mingle!

It is more important to attend a club's social hour than the meeting itself. When pressed for time, you'll make more contacts and perhaps even learn more if you arrive promptly for the social period and cut out before the speaker.

What is the best way to work a room? Make a sport of it. The following six-point plan of attack works best.

1. **Think gamesmanship.** Make a "Beat-the-Clock"game out of mingling and see how many potential alliances you can make at each club meeting.

2. **Surpass personal best.** Prepare for the game of meeting potential alliances like a runner psychs up for a race. Aim for your personal best each outing, always increasing the number of "contacts per allotted minutes" from your last performance.

3. **Double-team them.** Don't congregate with people you know. To make meeting new people easier, consider working a room with an ally. You can introduce each other to potential linkages.

4. **Use zone coverage.** If several people from the same company attend an event, spread out at various tables. This forces you to meet more people. Often a company will "buy a table" of eight or ten seats. It is fine to symbolically buy the table, but ask to distribute the people to different tables.

5. **Go head-to-head.** When seating is unassigned, choose your table with purpose. Read the room as if you were San Francisco 49ers Quarterback Joe Montana studying the defense. Size up the people sitting at the various tables and choose the table with the most potential alliances. Even be "sly"—just happening to sit with someone you have been wanting to meet.

6. **Take rookies under your wing.** Appoint yourself unofficial welcome wagon. Watch for newcomers, visitors, and other disoriented folks. Greet them and make them feel at home. You probably will make some friends for life.

Principle Four: Let a Staffer Be Your Guide

Do your homework before joining a group by forming a linkage with the key staff person. Large, established groups often pay someone to handle logistics and finances. This person can be a valuable ally, because he or she can suggest which committees would be beneficial and which to avoid. A staff person also can get you quick information you desire about club members and programs. Plus, if your name is on the staff person's mind, you may be recommended when others are seeking information in your area of specialization.

Principle Five: When in Doubt, Join Membership

To gain the favorable attention of the group's power structure, join the membership committee. Membership dues are the lifeblood of local clubs like the chamber of commerce, Rotary Club, and many professional associations. The person who adds cash to the coffers gets the attention of those in charge.

One public relations agency president rose quickly to the board of directors of a chamber of commerce through the membership route. She joined the chamber's membership committee and sent a letter to all her clients selling them on the benefits of becoming part of the chamber. She met with many key board members and sought their advice on "how she could help the chamber." When the chamber sold tables for major luncheon events, she bought a table and resold the seats to clients. It was hard work, but she rose through the ranks. And she won a great number of new clients—all influential chamber board members—from the strategy too.

Principle Six: Visibility through Volunteering

Whether it's politics, charitable arts groups, or medical-related organizations, there is always a need for people who can raise funds. These are the folks who garner the attention of the leaders.

Once entrenched in a committee, volunteer for a specific project. Then use it as a vehicle to conduct informational interviews with key people inside and outside the organization.

All Doors Open to a Volunteer

Do you have a particular interest or area of expertise that would benefit an organization? Suggest to the board that you'd like to form a task force to investigate it. In effect you will be forming your own committee. Then use the task force to interview board members and other potential linkages about the issue. Breakfast and lunch with allies you are nurturing to gain their input. Attend the board meeting to issue your task force report. You may even want to offer to turn the task force findings over to the newsletter editor so the membership can learn more.

You also can gain visibility by volunteering your services to the program chairman. That person has a year's worth of speakers to book, and you'll be taking weight off his or her shoulders if you offer to fill a slot—or if you volunteer your boss or client to serve as a speaker.

When you join a group, ask the program chairman for the list of upcoming topics to be covered and the ones for which speakers are needed. Crisis public relations was the topic one professional organization wanted to cover. Scheduled several months into the year, the program chairman hadn't even begun to contact potential speakers when she got a call from a well-known public relations man who had years of experience. The man got the speaking engagement and the visibility as someone who can adeptly put out fires under pressure.

Informational Interviewing Techniques

We all know that people like to give advice. That's why everyone prefers to serve on an advisory committee—not to mention that it involves much less work than a real committee. Use this to your advantage. Many people who don't have time to meet with you probably have time to meet with a representative of their club or organization to give advice on certain issues. This gets you in the door. Once you are in the door, make good use of the person's time.

And Work Hard, But Not Too Hard

Work toward becoming a leader of the group, but avoid assignments that require maximum work with minimum reward.

Principle Seven: If Your Group Doesn't Exist, Form It

When you discover that an organization doesn't exist in an area where you want to form linkages, take advantage of a golden opportunity and form such a group. When you establish a club, there is no need to work your way up into the leadership—you *are* the leadership.

Catherine Wambach and Kevin Leap were partners in an advertising and public relations agency specializing in high-tech. When they wanted to join a group to meet high-tech marketing executives, they found no such group existed. So they helped form one. In less than a year, their Computer and Electronics Marketing Association had nearly one hundred members and an average breakfast meeting attendance of forty people. Through their efforts to obtain speakers and publish the monthly newsletter, Wambach and Leap have formed linkages throughout the expansive high-tech community.

In New Orleans, the competition between hotels is very heated. But that didn't stop Michele Hogan Schmidt, public relations director at the Sheraton New Orleans Hotel and Towers, from helping to found a luxury hotel public relations group. Meetings are small and informal, usually with eight in attendance. The public relations directors discuss common problems, share tips on publicity opportunities, and circulate good industry ideas they have discovered.

Forming linkages has paid off. When a travel writer from *Business Travel News* stayed at the Sheraton, Schmidt convinced the writer to visit some of the other group members, such as Michele Vachon of the Windsor Court Hotel. Similar groups have now formed in other cities.

Deborah Purdy, a marketing executive, wanted to join a small business networking group, but she didn't like its practice of mandatory attendance and high dues. She found a few other disgruntled would-be members and formed her own group, making her own rules. Within three months, the organization was thirty-five members strong and Purdy earned two contracts for her company through the contacts she made.

Top Self-Marketing Secrets

Seven Principles for Maximizing Membership Opportunities

1. Strive to join groups in which you are one of the few representatives from your profession or corporate rank, rather than organizations comprised solely of professional colleagues.
2. Let someone convince you to join the group. Use him or her as an ally to become a leader of the group, but avoid assignments that require maximum work with minimum reward.
3. It is more important to attend the social hour than the meeting itself.
4. Do your homework before joining a group. Begin by forming a linkage with the key staff person.
5. Joining the membership committee is a smart way to gain the favorable attention of the group's power structure.
6. Seek out high-visibility assignments, such as ad-hoc committees that report to the board of directors.
7. When you discover that an organization doesn't exist in an area where you want to form alliances, take advantage of a golden opportunity and form such a group.

3

And the Winner Is...
How to Tastefully Exploit Your Award-winning Status

Imagine the envious applause as you accept an award your peers wish were going on *their* office wall. You can only bask in the glow so long, but if you capitalize on your new nonmortal status, you can make this award one that keeps on winning.

Surprisingly, it's not always the superior work that wins, but that which is packaged to catch the judge's eye. Learn how to market your entry by joining an organization's awards committee (a thankless job, but a guaranteed no-waiting-list group). You'll learn deadlines, criteria, and the frightening way awards are selected. Quickly.

Prepare for Fame

Most busy professionals want to enter awards competitions, but they don't make their move until deadline day. Then they scurry around the office trying to assemble all the pieces of the entry and quickly fill out the entry form—giving it little thought. Many awards judges have rendezvoused with last-minute entrants on freeway off-ramps as they head to the judging site.

Find out when the awards competitions you want to enter will be held and start preparing months ahead of time. As you work on a special project, think "award entry." Make notes as you go to remind yourself of the specific project obstacles you had to overcome so you can include them in your application. In addition to the job file, create an award entry notebook. Put copies of the business or marketing plan, budget, and pieces of the project in the notebook so you have everything in one place when it's time to enter. Being prepared puts you ahead of the competition from the beginning.

How to Enter to Win

Here are five quick tips to help you win more than your fair share of awards.

1. The last shall be first. Most award entries describe what happened in the logical order of challenge, strategy, tactics, and results. Wrong, wrong, wrong. Remember those judges are very busy. It's much more powerful to tell the results up front—"doubled sales," "increased awareness 70 percent," "the most successful opening in the firm's history." Then describe the situation, painting as bleak a picture as possible. Finally, list the strategy and tactics you used to achieve this brilliance. People don't care how well you did it until they know how well you did.

When entering a national awards competition for providing public relations for local chapters of a psychiatric association, a public relations firm opened its entry with the cost equivalency of that public relations space if it had been purchased through advertising. The $9,000 the society invested for public relations was worth $47,000 in advertising dollars. What a savings! And it pointed out that the space it earned—for example, the front page of the lifestyle section in the newspaper—was prime space not even made available to advertisers.

2. Don't just tell, when facts can sell. Vague descriptions produce vague feelings. Vague doesn't win awards. Describe results in specific terms.

A writer entering a local awards program submitted an article, published by a major magazine, about a plastic surgeon's work to correct a little girl's congenital deformity. That's a nice coup, but what impact did that have on the subject of the story? The writer revealed that since the story was published, the physician had received a dozen calls from others afflicted by the defect. He went on to perform three more similar surgeries that turned around others' lives as a result of her article.

3. Look for flip quality. Be sure your presentation has the "flip quality" of a great magazine. The *New Yorker* is a magazine with excellent flip quality. Between the great cartoons and dramatic ads, you can enjoy the magazine immensely just by flipping through the pages. Your award entry should do the same.

When writing your justification, use bold headlines and bulleted points so that the judges can see important points quickly. Time is limited; don't make them wade through gray matter to find out why you are deserving of recognition.

Whenever possible, use originals of your work—not photocopies—in your presentation. Spice up one- or two-color entries with colored backgrounds.

4. Who, what, when, where, why, and wow! More than just the facts, ma'am. What is the something extra? It should make the judges say, "Wow, this deserves an award!"

For a restaurant, one of the best "awards" is a favorable restaurant review. Being reviewed is always risky, because your eatery may get panned. But Richard Giboney, vice president of marketing for Restaurants Unlimited, believes that it is a risk worth taking. He has had a 100 percent success rate in getting his collection of specialty restaurants reviewed, and he uses the "wow" factor to get the reviewer's attention. "We have sent fact sheets printed on an apron or an invitation attached to a box with one of our chocolate whiskey cakes," says Giboney. "We never want to be ignored."

5. We shall overcome. Part of your entry should be a thirty-word explanation of the obstacles you overcame. Knowing budget or time constraints will persuade judges to pin the ribbon on your project over a more-impressive entry that bears no rhyme or reason.

Another award-winning restauranteur is Scarlett Rabalais, a hot dog stand owner. Scarlett received a Giraffe Commendation from the Giraffe Project Research Office, a volunteer foundation that recognizes people who stick their necks out to help others. Not only does she hire retired persons, who most businesses would consider unemployable, Scarlett has had to fight various zoning laws to run her collection of hot dog stands. She received national publicity after winning the award, including a feature story in the *USA Today Weekend* magazine.

How to Take a Bow

Once you've won, be advised that using your trophy as a hood ornament is out, but subtle ballyhooing is definitely in. Send a news release to the local media, professional trade journals, alumni newsletters, and your hometown newspaper, and write an article about the award for your employee newsletter. Then mail the newspaper clipping to customers and potential clients, and route them to your superiors. Circulate copies of congratulatory letters you receive to your boss and subordinates, with a "we won" memo.

Michelle M. Mueller, assistant vice president of Titan Linkabit, capitalizes on her growing recognition after an award victory by offering to give a speech based on her expertise. "We deal in government computer contracts and are judged on our community presence. Using awards as a springboard for that helps me do my part," she says.

After winning one award, Mueller was asked to give a talk to the chamber of commerce on marketing for small businesses. She also hosted a seminar at her company on enhancing communication style though improving personal appearance, which resulted in a *Los Angeles Times* feature story.

Mueller also highlights award information on her résumé and submits the updated version to her superiors prior to her semiannual review.

Along with listing the awards on your résumé, add the words "award winning" to your company's brochure or collateral sales pieces.

Putting Fame on Display

In addition to displaying an award plaque in your office, have a duplicate made for your boss or a key associate. Or give an extra copy with both of your names on it to an outside firm who played an instrumental part in your receiving it—the subcontractor, consultant, graphic artist, or printer. Your name in lights on their wall will earn extra recognition for you from everyone who walks into their office.

Margaret McAllister, of McAllister Communications, produced an award-winning community newsletter for a major medical center. She had professional photographs taken of the award and the publication's masthead that listed the contributors' names. The photos were mounted and sent with a thank you note to all of her freelancers. Next time she asks for their participation, you can bet they'll be willing to help.

When potential clients want to see samples of your work, casually point out award-winning projects. Whether it's a boss or a customer, a third-party endorsement of your work will increase your value.

In addition to making sure the award has a prominent home in your office, consider hanging a large photograph of the actual work in your company's entryway. An architect's prize-winning schematic, a writer's award-winning article (with the colorful cover of the magazine), or an engineer's noteworthy design all make interesting artwork and a centerpiece for discussion. Why buy a Rembrandt when you can tout your fame and create artwork as well?

Hold Your Own Competition

You know how much you like to be recognized, so why not encourage your company to sponsor a competition of its own? Giving out awards earns you recognition from the entrants as well as from follow-up publicity citing you and your company as the sponsor.

A local Society of Psychiatric Physicians holds an annual media awards luncheon to recognize reporters who cover psychiatric topics. A letter that invites all media to participate by sending in copies of their articles on this important topic makes reporters evaluate the coverage they're giving to the subject. A special luncheon held to recognize their work gives the psychiatrists and their public relations firms an opportunity to meet the reporters and to thank them for their interest.

After the competition, many of the winning newspapers and radio and television stations run short stories about their awards, once again mentioning the organization.

When it comes to awards, it's not what you win, it's how you play the fame.

Top Self-Marketing Secrets

Tips on Tastefully Exploiting Awards

1. As you work on a special project, begin to think about entering award competitions. Create a separate award entry notebook.

2. Remember the judges are too busy to scrutinize every entry. Put the results up front so they can't be missed.

3. Be sure your presentation has the "flip quality" of a great magazine. Spice up the entry with color.

4. Garner publicity on your award and then mail the newspaper clippings to existing and potential customers.

5. Have duplicates of the award made to give to others who were instrumental in the project.

6. Hold a competition of your own. Giving awards to others earns you recognition among the entrants.

4

Pleased to Media You
Nine Lessons on Becoming the Quoted Expert

Some say Red Adair had a burning desire to be famous. His exploits were featured in countless television news shows, newspaper stories, and magazine articles. John Wayne even made a movie about his life. If your oil well is on fire anywhere in the world, who would you call? Everyone in the oil industry knows the answer is Red Adair. Probably no one else even comes to mind.

Who is the Red Adair in your line of work? When your customers describe you, do they use terms that set you apart from your competition? Customers trust a consultant who does one thing and does it very well. You need to determine a specialized area of your business in which you would like to be an expert. Invest time and energy in researching this area. Then constantly strive to earn media coverage that positions you as this authority. If you follow the steps outlined in this chapter, you will be spotlighted in the media as the expert. It's unlikely Meryl Streep or Jack Nicholson will be signed to make a movie about your life, but you never know.

Below are several career choices that lend themselves to this positioning strategy. For each occupation, the positioning choices are limitless. You must determine the type of people you most want as customers. Usually your best prospects are people a lot like you. Then brainstorm what topics that appeal to you would most appeal to them.

Why should they buy from you when they could buy from anyone? Because you are the expert. For each of the following occupations, one of an unlimited number of positioning choices is listed to give you concrete examples.

Occupation	Positioning
Accountant	New hotel feasibility authority
Architect	New designs in office towers expert
Bank officer	Small business banking expert
Doctor	Sports injury and orthopedic surgeon
Financial planner	Financial strategist for single career women
Gym owner	Bodybuilding and weight training authority
Insurance agent	Local expert on needs of single parents
Lawyer	High-stakes divorce authority
Men's clothier	Widest selection of the latest European suits
Real estate agent	Executive relocation specialist

Whatever your expertise, be prepared to sum up your positioning in as few words as possible. A theater producer once said that if you can't write your idea down on the back of a business card, you don't have much of an idea. The same holds true for positioning. It must be short and simple so referral sources, potential customers, and the media can remember it. Use the rule of thumb most big advertising agencies use when creating billboards: seven words or less. If billboard writers use more than seven words, drivers whizzing by will miss the message. Don't let important audiences miss your positioning message as they whiz through life.

If you have the right stuff, contact the *Directory of Experts, Authorities, and Spokespersons.* This book is in its seventh edition and is the number one source for reporters, editors, news producers, and talk show producers. If you are an expert, be sure you are included in this book.

Lesson One: I'm an Expert, My Telephone Index Card Proves It

One of the most precious possessions a journalist has is his or her telephone card file. Newspaper reporters, television assignment editors, and talk show producers use these files daily to find interview subjects. Don't wait for them to discover you and include your name in their file. Send them a card that lists you as a subject expert.

The key to this technique is to think *subject*. What are your areas of expertise that relate to your positioning? Create one or two different cards, by heading, to send to the media.

After the subject, list your name, title, and the organization you represent. The next line is the most critical. Include a few words about your credentials in this topic—what your organization does, what you do with the organization, awards you've won, relevant accomplishments, books you've written, or the cause you represent. Include both your work and home telephone numbers. Most will only call you during regular hours, but remember that news is an around-the-clock business. Being available is a key to becoming a quoted expert. Below are some hypothetical cards that could be sent to the media.

Architecture
Frank L. Left
Principal, Left and Gauche Architects
Designer of more than 100 office buildings
Work: (204) 555-1234
Home: (204) 555-5678

Baseball Cards
Lotta Gumm
Owner, The Baseball Card Store
Has a personal collection of 1 million cards
Work: (303) 555-1234
Home: (303) 555-5678

Bodybuilding
I. M. Fitt
Owner, Fitt Family Health Centers
Former state champion weightlifter
Work: (212) 555-1234
Home: (212) 555-5678

Divorce
Marvin Bailey
Attorney at Law
Popular speaker on "How to Handle Your Own Divorce"
Work: (616) 555-1234
Home: (616) 555-5678

Mortgage Rates
Hedda Numbers
Vice President, First American Bank
Head of all real estate loans
Work: (415) 555-1234
Home: (415) 555-5678

Tax Law
Seymour DeDuckshuns
Managing Partner, D & C Accounting
Tax CPA for 15 years
Work: (312) 555-1234
Home: (312) 555-5678

The next step is to determine which media people should receive the telephone cards. This depends on your customer base. If you deal with local customers, you should seek to attract local coverage. If your customers come from the surrounding region, then regional coverage is appropriate. And, naturally, if you handle a national or international clientele, then you can seek this same level as a quoted authority.

A case in point. In the 1988 Olympics, the sporting world's attention was focused on the 100-meter dash. The Canadian sprinter Ben Johnson defeated Carl Lewis of the United States, only to be stripped of his title when a drug test revealed that he was using steroids.

Steroids became a hot topic with the media. Journalists quickly scrambled on all levels to find experts who could comment on these performance-enhancing drugs. On the national level, an "NBC Nightly News" or a *Newsweek* magazine would go with a national authority such as a researcher with a pharmaceutical lab. On the local level, the local television news and daily newspaper would attempt to localize the story. If you were I. M. Fitt, a local fitness gym owner who could articulately describe the pros and cons of steroids, you would be an excellent candidate to be the quoted expert. Editors and reporters would find you because your card was in their file.

After you have determined your appropriate level—local, regional, national, or international—put together a mailing list. Send each journalist on your list one card per subject along with a short note. Here is an example from I. M. Fitt, our local exercise gym owner.

Date
Fitt Family Health Center
1234 Main Street
Anytown 98765

Mr. Perry Black
News Editor
Daily World
P.O. Box 111
Anytown 98765

Dear Mr. Black:

If you need a source on bodybuilding, weightlifting, fitness training, or steroids, please feel free to call me.

As a former state weightlifting champion and the owner of a local fitness gym, these are areas where my expertise may be of value to you.

It would be a pleasure to provide you with information or to suggest others who could help. Enclosed are a telephone index card and a business card for your use.

Yours cordially,

I. M. Fitt
Owner

Enclosure

The key is to be short and to the point. Stress what is in it for them. Promise not only to provide information but also assistance in finding others who can help. This demonstrates that your interests are not totally self-serving. And when the media calls, come through with good information and good contacts. Be bold in what you say, because boring interviews will not be used. Also, respect journalists' deadlines and keep them holy. Always get back to a media call within one hour. Train the people who work with you to red flag such calls and put you in touch immediately. When a journalist is on deadline, often the first expert she can reach is the one who gets used.

Telephone index cards work. Suzan Berns, media relations director for the San Francisco Jewish Community Federation, had a bright idea when she printed up Day-Glo-colored cards. She emblazoned just the word "Jewish" on the card tab. Although she admits that people laughed when they first saw it, she knows it made her stand out in their phone files. An article in the *San Francisco Chronicle* was among the results of the eye-shocking card.

Back to who should receive the cards. Let's examine the local level; however, the same rules of thumb apply to the national level. In those cases, just substitute Ted Koppel's "Nightline" for your local TV news, *USA Today* for your town's newspaper, and the "Oprah Winfrey Show" for the hometown interview show. Reporters change jobs frequently, so send new cards out every six months.

1. Newspapers and Magazines

The first people to include are the beat reporters who cover your industry. Check the bylines of the stories that involve your industry to determine who regularly covers these stories. Obtain the names of all of the editors from the newspaper. The steroids-at-the-Olympics story could have been handled by one of many departments: news, features, medicine, fitness, or sports. Make sure that they all have your telephone index card. Also be sure to include all of the columnists, from financial to sports, on your mailing list. Even if your expertise is baseball cards, you could be just the source the financial columnist needs for that story on offbeat investments.

2. Television

The next people to include are the television assignment editors. These are the people who determine what stories will be covered and who will do the interviews. You can obtain their names by calling the television stations. If you are really ambitious, you will include all of your town's television reporters. Each has a say in whom he or she will interview as an expert in a story. Does the station have an interview show? If so, get the name of the producer and send your telephone index card.

3. Radio

Then call the radio stations and ask for the names of everyone who works in news. Most stations will have only one or two people handling news. They rarely leave the station, but sometimes they conduct telephone interviews. In most major metropolitan areas, there will be one or two stations that have a real news staff that does on-the-scene interviews. By all means give every news staffer a card. Find out the names of producers for the radio interview and public affairs shows. Do not send the card to the on-air host unless that person also produces the show.

Lesson Two: Don't Wait for the Media to Call You

Now that you have a spot in all of the journalists' telephone index files, you can sit back and wait for them to call. Right? Wrong! Think like a reporter and an assignment editor if you want to become the quoted authority.

When Ben Johnson was disqualified, our would-be exercise expert I. M. Fitt should have been on the phone to the local television assignment editors immediately. The conversation would go something like this.

Fitt: Hello, is this the Eyewitness News assignment desk?

Desk: Yes it is, how can I help?

Fitt: My name is I. M. Fitt. I own the Fitt Family Health Centers. Perhaps you might be interested in a local angle on Ben Johnson's being disqualified from the Olympics. If you are, I am a former state weight-lifting champion and I know a lot about steroids. I would be happy to provide your reporter with information or an interview.

Desk: We might be doing something on the Johnson story. How do you know about steroids?

Fitt: We teach seminars on the pros and cons of steroids at our gym. Many young football players and track stars don't know steroids are time bombs that cause early death.

Desk: Let me get your phone number. We may use you.

Scan the morning newspaper. Examine what is on this week's cover of *Time* and *Newsweek*. Whatever is making the headlines is good material for local news, but they need hometown experts. This is where you come in.

Coauthor Henry represented Target Stores when the company introduced the retail chain with eight simultaneous store openings in California. Although the chain was well-known in the Midwest, awareness was virtually nil on the West Coast. Henry's job was to keep Target in the news for eight weeks before the opening.

The first few weeks were relatively easy. Henry worked with the media to cover various angles including mass hirings, eight simultaneous remodeling projects, scholarship competitions, and charitable donations to art institutions. After five weeks the media began to get tired of hearing that the Target Stores were going to open.

So Henry scanned the daily headlines for an idea. That week a national truck strike began, and Henry checked how it would affect the local Target openings. Store officials said the truck strike would slow them down but not stop the openings. Henry arranged for a Target store manager to be interviewed on the evening news with that local comment on the national trucking strike story.

Lesson Three: A Primer on News Releases

Some say the news release is dead. Actually, it isn't even sick. When you want to position yourself as an expert with the media, the news release can play an important role. A news release is a useful tool for announcing promotions, upcoming events, and new products. We call this the Chinese Water Drip Torture Approach to publicity: little drips and drops of articles that mention your name.

News releases work where there is a section of a newspaper or magazine that devotes itself to publishing little blurbs culled from the stacks of news releases. So by all means, use this self-marketing strategy. But a news release is the wrong approach to garner a big interview, which is the publicity jackpot.

News releases don't result in big interviews or features because the media knows you mass produced them and sent them to everybody. To feature you, the media wants an exclusive, a news angle offered to them and them alone. To do this, use a query letter. Less is more with query letters to the media. In less than one page you tell what the story idea is and why you are the best person to interview. Chapter 7 goes into how to write a query letter in more detail.

So what do you want, quantity or quality? Little name mentions or a big splash? The answer is both. They both serve to position you as the expert. The more times your name is seen, the more recognized your name will become. To help you with your self-marketing, we offer a sample news release.

CONTACT: Henry J. DeVries or Diane Gage
              (619) 755-5151   (619) 297-2400

10/3/90

NEWS FROM
SELF-MARKETING SECRETS

PUBLICITY WRITING TIPS GIVEN AT SAN DIEGO WORKSHOP

SAN DIEGO - Basic guidelines for writing and
sending out news releases were suggested today at
a publicity-writing workshop by Henry DeVries and
Diane Gage, authors of SELF-MARKETING SECRETS.

"A key to getting your news releases used by
the media is to follow journalistic style,"
DeVries said. "News releases should be typed,
double spaced on 8 1/2-
by-11-inch paper. Each paragraph should be
indented five spaces and consist of 35 to 45
words," he said.

"Including the name and telephone number of
whom the media can contact for more information
is a must," said Gage. "Also use the heading 'NEWS
FROM...' so the media will easily know the source
of the information."

The heading information should include the day,
month, and year it is being given to the media.
If the material should be held for release until
a certain time, clearly note this on the first
page. This is sometimes used for news releases
about speeches, like commencement addresses, and
major announcements.

(more)

SELF-MARKETING SECRET
ADD ONE

According to newspaper great Joseph Pulitzer, the three most important elements of journalistic writing are accuracy, accuracy, and accuracy. Carefully check the spelling of first and last names, addresses, figures, and grammar.

Have at least two people proofread all news releases before you distribute them. Use the same major references as the media, which are an ASSOCIATED PRESS STYLE BOOK, the telephone white pages, and WEBSTER'S COLLEGIATE DICTIONARY.

Write in what is called the inverted pyramid style. The most important information should be at the beginning and proceed in descending order of importance. A good news release should be written so that if space is tight, it can be cut from the bottom up and still make sense.

Keep it short. Never use more than two pages unless you have to, and rarely use more than three pages. If you have more to say, attach a narrative fact sheet that journalists refer to as a "backgrounder."

The writing should be factual and not promotional. Avoid excessive adjectives that try to hype you or the organization. Be sure to translate jargon into lay language.

(more)

SELF-MARKETING SECRET
ADD TWO

"Editors like wide margins at the top and along the sides so they can write in changes," said DeVries. "Other rules of thumb include don't split paragraphs between pages and put '(more)' at the bottom center of all but the last page."

Place a heading flush left in all capital letters at the start of each new page. On the line under the heading, put ADD ONE for the second page, ADD TWO for the third page and so on. At the end, put three number signs centered, like this:

# # #

Lesson Four: For Every Media Topic There Is a Season

You do not need psychic powers to predict the news. Certain stories appear with regularity. Sex, money, and health are the three topics that are always in style. If you can provide new information on these subjects, the media will welcome your input.

Other topics come in and out of style. Just like there are fashions in clothes and cars, there are fashions in news. To be a quoted authority, think not only news topic but also what is in style for this news season.

Here is a month-by-month list of news topics. Newspapers, magazines, television, and radio are looking for fresh spins on these ageless news pegs.

January	fitness, predictions, Super Bowl
February	romance
March	spring training
April	baseball
May	moms
June	weddings, graduations, dads
July	vacations, Fourth of July
August	hot weather
September	back to school, football
October	World Series, Halloween
November	elections, Thanksgiving
December	holidays, year-end wrap-ups, resolutions

Another predictable aspect of media coverage is the anniversary story. For example, major news events are re-examined after intervals of one, ten, twenty, twenty-five, and thirty years. Not only does history repeat itself, so does the news. Barry Gurley, a district manager with the Independent Order of Foresters, received extensive coverage in 1989 when he organized a disaster relief team to help victims of Hurricane Hugo. One year later he was still in the news.

Despite its being 200 miles inland, Hurricane Hugo pounded the town with 135 mile-per-hour winds. Gurley's volunteers removed damaged trees threatening the homes of the elderly, disabled, and poor. His month-long campaign helped more than

800 families and attracted more than 1,000 volunteers from around the country. The local television stations, radio programs, and daily newspaper all interviewed Gurley on the hurricane's anniversary.

A quick scan of the following list will help you see what other anniversaries will be making news. Check the list and brainstorm how you could tie-in with these anniversaries and others.

April 4, 1993	25th anniversary of Martin Luther King assassination
November 22, 1993	30th anniversary of Kennedy assassination
June 6, 1994	50th anniversary of the D-Day Invasion
July 20, 1994	25th anniversary of first moon landing
August 6, 1995	50th anniversary of Hiroshima atom bomb
December 31, 1995	25th anniversary of the official breakup of the Beatles

Lesson Five: Be an Industry Expert

"Always avoid being self-serving" is a message we can't stress enough. You are there to promote your organization or cause, but the stories you will be interviewed for will not be on this. The reporters will want to interview you about a subject that pertains to your industry or area of expertise. The payoff is the mention of your name and organization.

To promote his public relations agency, Henry circulated his telephone index card to the local media. Some of the subjects he was interviewed on included

- public relations ramifications of the Exxon Valdez oil spill in Alaska
- marketing trends to watch for in the 1990s as the baby boomers age
- how small business should attract Hispanic customers
- time management tips for busy executives

In each instance Henry was not directly promoting his business. He was providing industry-wide information. In his favorite interview, he was asked what public relations advice he would give Ivana Trump after her split with Donald. The reporter was looking for fun quotes, not a serious dissertation. Henry recommended that Ivana stay in the spotlight. "There are a number of different things Ivana could give of herself to improve her image. She could give out information. She could share what she knows, maybe give a seminar on how to get by on a budget. She could give of her time by helping over-privileged children. She could give of her talent by teaching a small-business seminar through her chamber of commerce. I don't recommend that she give money, because she has to watch her pennies now."

Lesson Six: The Three P's of Media Interviews

Many of these techniques will help you get interviewed once; to keep the media coming back to you as a valued source, you will have to give great interviews.

To help you be "oh so quotable," we believe in the three P's formula: prepare, promote, and perform. Prepare what you are going to say in advance. Promote your cause. And perform so your message gets through. Use the following checklist before any interview, from one minute on the local news to a full hour with Barbara Walters. This checklist was derived from the teachings of media interview specialist Joe Feurey, a former television news producer and currently president of Professional Communications Services of New York City.

Prepare
1. Determine what three points you want to make.
2. Always rehearse and say only what you plan to say.
3. Make your message really simple.
4. Repeat it over and over.

Promote
1. Remember that you are there to promote your cause.
2. Don't think of this as a search for the truth.
3. Say only what you plan to say.
4. Work in the name of your organization or cause frequently.

Perform
1. Realize that radio and TV are performance media.

2. Keep in mind that the more prepared you are, the more trustworthy you look.
3. Smile and project lots of energy.
4. Build performance skills through rehearsal.
5. Pretend you aren't afraid and that you enjoy the experience.

Lesson Seven: Nine Surefire Ways to Give Good Media Interviews

What else does it take to give great interviews? Here are some excerpted tips we really like that were compiled by Gallen Associates.

1. Rank the reporter number one.

   ■ When you get calls from reporters, assume they are on deadline. If you're in a meeting or out of town, have a designated person contact them immediately.

2. Establish ground rules.

   ■ Offer the writer a bio with the correct spelling of your name, your title, and a clear description of your responsiblities.

   ■ Assume everything that you say will be in print. Some input is better than not having any input at all.

3. Get to know the reporter, the publication, and the topic.

   ■ Review a recent issue of the publication before the interview.

   ■ Try to determine how familiar the reporter is with the topic.

   ■ Ask the writer the objective of the story before you start.

   ■ Use the fax machine to provide follow-up information, especially for potentially confusing information.

4. *Talk* to the reader. Avoid technical jargon but don't be afraid to be educational.

- Use examples that create *word pictures* to make points easy to understand.

5. Keep your promises.

- Get follow-up information to reporters on time, before the deadline.
- If you are going to follow up with visuals, ask the reporter the preferred format.

6. Don't just give answers—give good answers.

- Don't jump to respond.
- If you can't back up a fact, don't use it.

7. Use "journalism etiquette."

- Never say "thank you." A good reporter who produces a balanced story is doing his or her job.
- However, it is appropriate to acknowledge a "job well done" and to send a note to that effect.
- You can ask the reporter to restate what you have said. Don't demand.
- Don't ask for an advance copy of the article.
- If you want to take a reporter to lunch or to underwrite the reporter's transportation, be sensitive to company policy.

8. Be a resource—not just a source.

- If you want to build a relationship with the reporter, prove you are a good source. Think of other articles or books that may help the reporter with the article.
- If the reporter is on the wrong track or has wrong information, don't be afraid to point it out gingerly.

9. Minimize distractions.

- Dedicate time to the interview and not to putting out fires.

- Don't interrupt the "flow" of the interview to take phone calls.

Lesson Eight: Handling a Crisis

One day it's going to happen. It might be a lawsuit. Maybe an accident at your place of business. Or perhaps a labor dispute. Want it or not, a crisis will bring the media to you and thrust you into the spotlight.

Often the first reaction is to say "no comment." This is the worst thing you could ever say, short of a full admission of wrongdoing. Such a comment is condemning, as it implies you have something to hide. The media and the public will assume you are guilty. If your goal is to postpone comment until you can assemble facts, there is another phrase you can use.

If you are ever asked to comment before you are ready, say this: "It would be premature to speculate at this time." This is a phrase often used by a public relations executive for one of America's biggest railroads whenever he is dispatched to a train wreck. His goal is to express concern—not blame or shame—and the intent to find out the cause of the wreck. Tell the media that you are greatly concerned about the issue, it has assumed top priority, and all resources are being used to assess the situation.

Many reporters will admit privately that you will be treated much better by the media if you use this approach. We all have bosses to report to, and so do journalists. Media bosses put pressure on reporters to get interviews. Even if all you can say is that it's premature to speculate, you are helping them out.

Remember that you need to make the best of a bad situation. If handled right, you can turn it into millions of dollars worth of publicity. That's what Robert Vicino did when his pet project, reuniting King Kong and the Empire State Building, went bananas.

In honor of the fiftieth anniversary of the premiere of the film *King Kong,* Empire State Building owner Harry Helmsley financed Vicino's efforts to have a giant, inflatable Kong scale this New York landmark in April 1983. This eight-story-high ape was the latest creation of Vicino's, who invented the advertising medium of cold air giant inflatables. Previously concentrating on twenty-foot-high beverage cans, Vicino hoped the stunt would cause other advertisers to go ape over his inflatables.

Vicino planned to surprise the Monday morning New York commuters, but all was not well with the gorilla of his dreams. A building bolt tore an eighteen-inch gash in Kong's vinyl as inflation began in the predawn hours. What then would have been an interesting promotion turned into a week-long international media event as Vicino's workers valiantly tried to turn a sagging piece of plastic into the menacing ape of movie lore.

Vicino would have preferred to work in secrecy until the inflatable was right. However, this wasn't an option in a city of 8 million that is also the media center of the world. So Vicino's public relations pro, Jack Mayo, worked out a media strategy. If there was good news to announce, Vicino handled it. If it was bad news, that was Mayo's job.

In countless interviews they said that they knew the kids of New York City were counting on seeing King Kong on top of the Empire State Building, and they would not quit until they came through for the kids. Kong was fully inflated in time for a crush of photo-snapping tourists that Saturday and Sunday. Vicino and Helmsley wanted Kong to remain for another week, but the police and mayor couldn't take another day of gridlock. Kong was moved to the great lawn of Central Park, a historic first for a commercial venture.

If the situation is ugly, get professional public relations help. You are about to be tried in the court of public opinion. Abraham Lincoln said that the man who defended himself in court had a fool for a client. You wouldn't go to court without legal counsel. Don't go into the court of public opinion without competent counsel as well.

Lesson Nine: Dealing with the Media during a Crisis

Roni Hicks, a public relations agency president with over twenty years of experience in the field, offers the following advice to her clients. In dealing with the media during a crisis, here are some specific steps to follow:

1. Provide media access to top executives. A senior executive must represent the company during a crisis. The words of a senior officer, someone who sets corporate policy, carry more weight than the same statements made by someone else.

2. Be open and candid. Withholding information or evading questions is almost sure to backfire. Journalists will learn the full story in one way or another. Overall media coverage will generally be fair if the agency sets forth company policies and procedures in their fullest form. Avoid at all costs the inclination to withhold information. The media will treat you worse after having obtained it through roundabout methods. This appears to the public as though the company is deliberately *covering up* some incompetence, or worse, malfeasance.

3. Present information from the viewpoint of the public interest, rather than from the company's interest. This is self-explanatory but important not to overlook, since we are accustomed to thinking in terms of company needs. Report news in the context of public interest, especially when it impacts public safety. Tell the whole story at once, if possible, rather than keeping it alive in the media while additional facts are announced or uncovered.

4. Respond to all media inquiries. Again, it is essential that the organization avoid the appearance of dodging media requests. If at all possible, maintain a log of media inquiries. This ensures that all requests for information are honored and provides a valuable record for later evaluation of and monitoring of the event's effects.

5. Never speculate. Guesswork can mistakenly be reported as fact, leading to misconceptions that are difficult to counter. Remember, too, that what you say may create expectations for which you will be accountable in the future. Make promises you know you can keep.

6. Remember past performance when developing responses. The organization's past record of performance will serve well in a crisis. Stress the positive where appropriate.

7. When you read a prepared statement, tell the truth without being too expansive—then be quiet. Wait for the press to ask questions before going into unnecessary detail. The reporters may not be interested, which will abbreviate the soon-to-be-published/aired sad tale.

8. Relax. When being interviewed, try not to view the reporter as an adversary. Mentally block out cameras and notebooks and concentrate on the message. Try to think of it as merely a dialogue between two people.

Top Self-Marketing Secrets

Nine Lessons on Becoming the Quoted Expert

1. Based on your occupation and positioning, choose a subject that interests you. Then become an expert in that area.

2. Send telephone index cards to the media listing yourself as an expert in your chosen subject.

3. Send a short note with the cards to appropriate newspaper, magazine, radio, and television people.

4. Don't wait for the media to call you. When you see a breaking story that you can comment on, call them so you will be the quoted authority.

5. Use news releases to obtain small articles that keep you or your organization's name in front of the public.

6. Figure out ways you can comment on predictable seasonal and anniversary stories that are certain to be covered by the media.

7. Avoid being self-serving when you are a resource to the media. Always be willing to help in any fashion, even if you and your organization are not the focus of the attention.

8. Learn how to give great interviews so the media will keep coming back for more.

9. If you don't know what to say during a crisis to the media, at least say that it would be premature to speculate. Never, ever say "no comment."

5

There's No Free Brunch
Do's and Don'ts of Media Bread Breaking

"Don't call us, we'll call you." No one will ever feed you that line as often as the media—that is, if you are green in how to win media friends and influence coverage.

You call a radio producer and ask him if he got that news release you sent. He says he doesn't remember, but he'll call you if he's interested.

You ask the business editor if she plans to run your story in the Sunday newspaper. She says it's not likely; you'll know if you see it.

You telephone the assignment editor at a TV news station to see if a crew will be covering your event. You get the perfunctory, "What was that again?" and who, what, when, and where questions, but no one shows up.

How do those savvy in media relations break down the barricade of "no thanks" and noncomittal responses that stream endlessly from the media? They treat them like colleagues and professionals and get to know them as people. They look, watch, and listen to *learn* who's doing what. They become genuinely interested in the stories covered, as well as their media contacts' career tracks. And, when the timing is right, they invite them for lunch or for coffee and, as they break bread, they banter about story ideas—some self-serving, many not.

It's not what you know, but *who* you know that counts when it comes to media relations. Count it a privilege whenever you get the opportunity to get to know a reporter, producer, editor, news director, or program manager on a personal basis. Display integrity, a nose for news, and a commitment to stories that will interest their readers, viewers, or listeners. Your chances of getting coverage increase once a media rep can match a name with a face.

Dorothy and Robert DeBolt, parents of twenty children—fourteen adopted and multihandicapped—have risen to international prominence as a top husband-wife speaking team, humanitarians, miracle workers, and pioneers in their fields of endeavor. They've received commendations from three presidents, and Dorothy is one of the few women to have received the nation's highest speaking award from the National Speakers Association. Millions have seen their Academy Award-winning film, *Who Are the Debolts?* or read their book, *19 Steps up the Mountain—The Story of the DeBolt Family.* Their notoriety all began because Dorothy made media friends.

When she and her first husband, Ted Atwood, adopted two Korean-Caucasian orphans in the fifties, it was the first such happening in their small town of Placerville, California. Taking full advantage of press and media interest in their human-interest story, Dorothy welcomed all interviews and furnished some of her own stories and letters to editors.

Later, when Dorothy formed her growing family into the Atwood Family Singers, she used her media contacts to help find fame through regular appearances on local television and even a national appearance on the "Tennessee Ernie Ford Show." From her small foothills town, she fed items to San Francisco's esteemed columnist, Herb Caen.

"I don't know whether Herb felt I had a certain ability with news 'hooks,' or whether he simply appreciated my audacity in submitting my items, but he used them," says Dorothy. "And the more he used them, the more our fame grew."

One of the most famous Caen quips came in the early sixties when Dorothy, a widow with seven children, booked her brood to sing at a local church. She fed an innocent remark by one of her sons to the columnist and the following appeared in the paper:

"Dorothy Atwood, the spunky Oakland widow who has organized her seven children into the Atwood Family Singers, took them to a party where an unknowing guest asked twelve-year-old

Marty: 'Where's your father?' 'We don't have one,' replied Marty. 'All we have is an unwed mother.'"

Through his column, Caen continued to follow Dorothy, covering her marriage to Bob DeBolt, their new adoptions, their movie, and their book. "Constant references in Herb's incredibly popular column are something for which a press agent would give his life. I got them for nothing!" says Dorothy. "The name recognition he provided me, and later Bob, our family, and our work, has played one of the greatest roles in any successes we have had in our careers."

Angles and Integrity Sell Stories

Even the strongest personal relationship with a columnist or reporter can't override an ill-conceived idea. Fresh angles and exclusives are what editors look for—even when they do know you by name. Don't wear out your welcome by pitching borderline ideas.

"Become a gatekeeper," says Craig Evans, director of public information for the Salvation Army in greater New York. "New York City is a tough market with many nonprofits vying for attention," he says. "I insure that any potential ideas I try to sell to the media are strong with the real potential of making it in print or on the air."

As a former newspaper reporter, Evans says that it's easy to sense when someone is throwing out an idea that he or she doesn't necessarily believe in just to try to get an organization's name in print. "Sincerity is important," he says. "Provide a commodity that a reporter needs."

When he worked on the other side of the editor's desk, Evans says that those who were able to break through to him were those who called in ideas first and followed up with a personal letter. "Reporters receive hundreds of news releases a day, and they become worthless after awhile," he says. "I'd rather get a phone call with a great idea, followed up with a handwritten note or personally drafted letter."

One warning: Know your reporters' and editors' deadlines. Don't call up late in the afternoon when a morning newspaper is jamming to close an issue. And forget trying to get through to television news at 4 P.M. when they're going crazy preparing for the 5 P.M. newscast.

Evans says he paid attention to those who had done their homework and had read what he'd been writing. "They had studied what I was covering and could speak intelligently about it, making references to stories I had done in the past," he says. "Yes there are egos involved and you have to appeal to them. But be sincere, not artificial."

Wooing Locals at a Brown-Bag Affair

Don't wait until you have a story that deserves coverage to meet your local media. One of the best ways to get to know local reporters who cover your community or your news beat (political, social, business, lifestyle) is to call them up and invite them to your place for a brown-bag lunch.

Bill the event as an informal gathering of members of your company who would like a chance to get to know the reporter and his or her needs better at a time convenient to the reporter. Host the deli-sandwich affair in your conference room and give the reporter a chance to describe his or her beat as well as those of associates, what is being looked for in stories, what has been done ad nauseum, and the type of stories that pique interest.

Take copious notes and refer to these how-to's the next time you are ready to write and send a query. Streamlining the information in exactly the right format for that specific media person will expedite an answer.

And while you are writing down business points, don't forget personal details like the reporter's alma mater, spouse's name, favorite sports, type of pet, vacation plans, and other interests. These can be icebreakers in conversation or reasons to communicate with the reporter on a more social basis. When you see a story on Switzerland in a magazine, clip it and send it to the reporter who is planning a vacation there next summer. Form media linkages like you would any other type of business connection. Most people treat the media differently from other businesspeople. Surprise! They're human, too!

Henry's former company, Roni Hicks & Associates, makes brown-bag lunches a monthly event. Regardless of how pressing it is to get a particular editor's interest in a story, one motto stands firm at Hicks: "No pitching on the first date." In other words, this is a nonpressured time for reporters. They don't have to worry about how to let account executives down easily when their story idea doesn't quite hit the mark. It is a time to get to know the idiosyncrasies of a particular radio or television show or newspaper section. But more important, it is an opportunity to get to know a reporter as a real person with interests, passions, hobbies, friends, and family. And it gives the reporter a chance to meet the public relations staff and get to know them personally.

Then when it is business as usual and the account exec makes the pitch call, it can be done on another level. Instead of immediately diving into describing the news angle, the exec can ask about the reporter's recent vacation or talk about the upcoming ball game. But the feeling of camaraderie always has to be genuine; there's nothing worse than a phony friend.

Diane and several other agency principals, all members of their professional association, Public Relations Society of America, take their show on the road. Every month or so, one member of the team arranges a meeting with a media representative. That person faxes the confirmation and meeting details to the others and the six public relations practitioners meet for breakfast, lunch, or an afternoon Coke for a roundtable discussion with the reporter, editor, or producer.

Even though you could consider these public relations professionals as competitors, they know that one good story doesn't preclude coverage of another. You can do the same with colleagues in your field. Sometimes there's strength in numbers. Joining forces to meet the media may encourage more coverage of your field and may encourage the idea of an industry round-up story in which several of you are quoted. Even more important, the industry itself gets a major recognition boost.

Taking Your Story National

Editors of national magazines, trade journals, and newspapers can't come to a brown-bag affair at your office, but you can certainly go to them. Face-to-face meetings are invaluable when you hit the big time.

If you've got a business meeting or conference to attend in a publication's headquarter's city, write ahead to the editor. Whenever possible, a month to six weeks lead time is preferable. State the week you will be in town and ask if you can drop by for ten minutes to present some story ideas. Then follow up with a phone call three or more weeks before you leave to set a meeting time. If you're down to the wire when you decide to pay an editor a visit, call instead of writing. Writing, however, is preferable because if you call the editor at a busy time, you are less likely to be put off if you are following up on a letter.

Having ideas for national media is essential. While information-gathering meetings are the ticket to local media relations, on a national level editors simply don't have the time. This is the one time when it's okay to put on the moves immediately. Show up at your meeting with a number of ideas honed specifically to that magazine or newspaper. Write them out in query letter form (See Chapter 7) so that the editor doesn't have to take notes and has an outline of your idea to pass along to other decision makers. Before you leave, give the editor your telephone index card that has a subject heading (e.g., Stockbroker, Jeweler, Dietitian) so that you can be found when your name has faded from memory but your subject area is remembered.

Once you are in the editor's office, chances are you'll have an opportunity to discuss other ideas that you haven't fleshed out. Running these by the editor will give you an inkling as to whether the idea has merit for a national story and if it is something you should pursue once you're back in the office.

Succeeding in Planned Media Interviews

In Chapter 4, we described how to write news releases, but here are a few more tips that will keep those precious relationships with your media contacts intact.

1. Don't send out mass mailings unless you have breaking news. Offering exclusives is a good way to build relationships with editors and reporters. Don't send the same idea to morning and evening papers if they are archrivals. Instead, choose one. If you really feel pressed, give them a deadline, "I'm offering this to you exclusively through 'X' date [a week is long enough] and will not propose it to another publication before then."

Patricia Dibsie, a reporter, says never give an idea to more than one paper, or they will see you as a traitor. "You owe it to yourself and the media to read newspapers and get a handle on various writers, so you can talk intelligently to the reporter and propose a just-right idea for him or her," she says. "Once you know the reporter's beat and style, call on the telephone to go over the idea before you send the release to see if there is interest or [to see] how you can streamline the idea. But if the reporter is on deadline, be thick-skinned enough to call back."

Exclusivity also goes for interview-format shows. They don't want to air topics that another has done or is planning to do. It's better to have one major piece of coverage than none. If you're sending out a press kit filled with a variety of fact sheets, bios, and backgrounders, be sure to send different news releases with different angles to competing media.

Rarely should you use the cookie-cutter approach for news releases. Streamline them to the reporter or producer. For newspaper exclusives, a query letter is probably the best bet. This letter talks directly to the reporter, immediately seems personal, and whispers exclusive. For television or radio, your query or release might read as though a TV audience was listening for thirty seconds.

2. Give the reporter background details to expand the story. Newspaper releases can be more detailed than television or radio ones. A health reporter may want to know if key individuals in your organization have been published in medical journals and will want to see background articles on that topic to lend credibility to the story. Business editors may want detailed financial reports or annual reports from previous years.

3. Avoid superlatives. The word expert is overdone. And don't think that you need to say you are the only one doing such and such. Reporters say that people often push too hard and use hysterical language, which makes the journalists naturally suspicious.

4. Be accurate. Don't make the story more than it is—you'll soon be found out and will only get away with it once.

5. Give all of the details that you can to save the reporter some steps. Betsy Eisele, who handles public relations for the Stevens Cancer Center at Scripps Memorial Hospitals in La Jolla, did that when she sent a health reporter a release about women with breast cancer having children after their diagnosis. The reporter said the query was perfect because it

- told about a nurse specialist in the field who would be coming to the Scripps Cancer Symposium
- included a local source who was doing the same work
- was a timely idea that had not been written about extensively
- offered a new way of looking at something
- suggested a San Diego woman who had been through breast cancer and became pregnant
- included background articles on the topic in professional journals, a flyer on the symposium, and a letter that outlined other interesting topics at the symposium
- was sent two months ahead of time

6. Be familiar with the format of the newspaper, radio show, or television show to which you are sending your idea. Maria Velasquez, host of "Saturday Morning" on KFMB-TV in San Diego, told of a recent experience in which a public relations professional contacted her about a segment idea. Velasquez agreed to do it. A few days later she received a message on her voice mail that said the client was available for an interview at 9 A.M. Thursday, so plan to bring a camera.

Since Velasquez's show tapes in the studio at 8 P.M. on Wednesday evening for airing Saturday morning, she knew that the public relations person had no clue as to what her show was all about. They were off to a rough beginning.

Velasquez cautions you not to pick up the phone or send a release or letter until you have thought out the segment and watched the program you target. Otherwise, you come across as uninformed and unaware.

7. Give the media plenty of lead time. For feature stories tied to an event, in which the window for meaningful coverage is narrow, give plenty of lead time to the media—a few months for print reporters and a month for TV and radio.

8. Avoid national recognition months. You may think National Kidney Month or Mental Illness Awareness Week is a media hook, but typically those predesignated months are a deterrent. Everyone is vying for space then—especially national organizations. Don't think you've missed the boat by not getting involved in these promotions. Instead, save your contacts and energy for a story that will make a difference at another time of the year.

9. Anticipate media stories. Highlight holidays on your calendar and become known for making yourself available for topics surrounding Christmas, Valentine's Day, Labor Day. Every newspaper wants a Halloween story, so think of something different for which you can be a spokesperson. One newspaper called a local psychiatrist to comment on whether people's personalities are reflected in the Halloween costumes they create.

10. Make yourself accessible to the media. One of the biggest problems reporters have is getting in touch with experts. While they appreciate that your work is important, they need time to cover the story without being put off or rushed. Train office staff to be responsive to media calls and to let you know when a reporter is on the line—even in the middle of a meeting. Reporters work on deadlines and need to be able to schedule an interview quickly and with the assurance that the expert won't cancel.

11. Whenever possible try to have all of the pieces of a story available at one place. If there is a visual at a manufacturing plant, can you do the interview rather than having the reporter and photographer or video crew make two stops—at the plant and your office? Don't think you're doing the media a favor by being interviewed. They are doing you a favor by exposing you and your business to thousands of people.

12. Think visuals for television. Have the *big picture* in mind when suggesting an idea to television. Suggest visuals to the reporter or producer in a cover letter when you send the query or news release. Think of more than *talking heads.* What scenes inside and outside your business depict the story?

Have ideas for background footage, called "B roll," that plays while the reporter is giving introductory remarks or closing the story or that illustrates a point you are making in the interview. For example, if you will talk about the safety of day care centers, know a few that will allow a cameraperson to come and shoot background film.

For talk shows shot in studio, visuals are a little different. What kind of props can you bring to illustrate a point? Do you already have a video that clearly demonstrates a particular part of the interview? Is there a client or customer who can accompany you to the studio to provide anecdotes?

13. Newspapers like art too. Newspapers are often desperate for art, so suggest visuals to them as well. Large unionized newspapers will always take their own photos. Determine if the newspaper will want to take photos and be prepared to be photographed while you are being interviewed. For smaller papers, send your own black and white, superior quality photos.

14. Respond immediately to media requests. If a reporter calls with a question, be expedient about getting back. If several hours pass and you don't have an answer, call to give a progress report. If you help a reporter meet a deadline, you'll become a fast friend.

Training to Be on Stage

The spokesperson for your company—you or another key individual—must be knowledgeable, articulate, and somewhat at ease in front of the camera or on the other side of a newspaper reporter's notepad. A person may be great at what he or she does, but that doesn't make him or her a good interviewee. Make sure that you choose the right person—it may not necessarily be you.

Make sure your spokesperson has enough to say. The golden rule of reporters is to have as much to say as possible in case they are forced to fill space or time. Statistics, summaries of studies, and personal stories are good for longer interviews. If the format allows, bring a client to the interview who can provide a testimonial about why a service or product is needed.

Role play with others in your company to prepare for the interview. For print media, have someone take notes as a reporter would. Then have that person report back to you what he or she heard. This will let you see how what you say is being interpreted. You'll suddenly realize why it's so easy to be misquoted. Be sure the pseudo-reporter practices using a variety of questions, not given in a set order. Even if they use questions you have provided, reporters will also make up their own and digress. And most reporters or producers will not give you their questions ahead of time so that you can practice. They are looking for spontaneity.

If you don't know the answer, be honest and say, "I don't think I can tell you that, but I can tell you…" If you stumble over your words, make a recovery—whether taped or live. Don't say, "Can we start over?" Just correct yourself immediately.

For a television interview, realize how succinct you must be. Try to get your point across in less than two minutes. Use a home video camera to tape practice segments, then play them back to critique. Above all, make sure you come across as knowledgeable and credible.

On-camera Pointers

Television interviews are the most unforgiving. That's when the entire package—presentation, voice, appearance, body language, and information—comes into play. Here are fifteen basic pointers for on-camera interviews.

1. Don't pay attention to the camera. Direct your comments to the reporter or host.

2. Wear a simple suit—plaids, checks, or houndstooth can be distracting.

3. Make sure that you are in tune with the angle the reporter is after, not just the angle you pitched—although in the best-case scenario, they are the same.

4. A cue card that lists major points to cover, a date, or an important phone number is permissible, but don't take other notes on camera with you.

5. If you ask in advance, important dates and phone numbers can be put on the teleprompter.

6. Speak in a medium-paced speed. Too fast is nerve-racking; too slow is boring.

7. Talk as you would to a client, not as though you are giving a speech. Avoid technical language and jargon.

8. Avoid space-fillers like "uh" and "um." In mock interviews, have someone sound a buzzer every time you revert to these crutches so that you can realize how often you use them.

9. Nail the topic to the wall with succinct, clear messages. "This is a new product that has been shown to…" If the viewer has that problem, they perk up. Don't back into a topic or you lose the viewer.

10. Break your topic down into three main points. This gives you an outline to work from and lets the reporter amd audience know where you're going and when you get there.

11. Have the latest facts and figures available. Don't give offhand answers. A reporter checks facts and needs to be able to trust you.

12. Have an historical perspective on your topic—still brief—to give depth if needed.

13. Cite studies or journals for newspaper interviews and for some radio interviews, but not for most television interviews. There just isn't time.

14. Prepare for the fact that you will probably not have the chance to review your quotes before the segment airs or the article runs.

15. Deliver what you promise. Once the reporter arrives to cover the story, make sure that you don't have hidden agendas.

Oh, yeah, before we forget, have fun! Media interviews can be a time to realize how much you do know and how terrific your product or service really is. You're the quoted expert, and if you're careful to maintain good relations with the media, you'll be quoted again and again.

Top Self-Marketing Secrets

Forging Media Bonds

1. Invite a media representative out to lunch to start building personal relationships.

2. Pitch fresh angles that won't wear out your welcome. Provide a commodity a reporter needs.

3. Know your reporters' and editors' deadlines.

4. Give newspaper columnists tidbits to fatten their daily space requirements.

5. Host an informal brown-bag lunch at your office and ask a reporter or producer to share insights.

6. Learn personal facts about media contacts to develop relationships that extend beyond your next story.

7. Take your media ideas on the road—visit national magazine and trade journal editors and radio and television talk show producers.

8. Prepare for media interviews by thinking of yourself as a package—face, voice, body, and information.

6

Six Publicity Secrets to Boost Sales
Why It's Illegal to Plow Fields with Elephants

Picture yourself bankrupt at the age of sixty-one. Now you know the problem faced by famed American showman Phineas Taylor "P. T." Barnum. Although penniless, he organized his first circus and humbly called it "The Greatest Show on Earth."

Music had Mozart. Mathematics had Einstein. And publicity had P. T. Barnum. Low on funds to promote his venture, Barnum used his creative genius to garner crowd-drawing newspaper coverage. No businessman in history, with the possible exception of Donald Trump, has craved publicity more than P. T. Barnum. When Barnum was near death, the editor of New York's *Evening Sun* did him a favor. He published his obituary before he died. When Barnum read four columns about his own death, he was delighted.

A century ago in small-town America, a daily highlight was the arrival of the train. Barnum would position an elephant pulling a plow alongside the train tracks, which always attracted a crowd and some free newspaper coverage. He also attracted the wrath of the farmers who didn't like elephants tearing up their fields. As a lasting legacy to Barnum's quest for publicity, it is illegal to plow fields with elephants in North Carolina. It seems Barnum did it one too many times.

To this day, when Barnum's creation—now called the Ringling Brothers Barnum and Bailey's Greatest Show on Earth—comes to town, you can count on an elephant appearing in the media.

Barnum had marketing instinct. He knew the publicity secret that all great self-marketers have come to know. Publicity offers impact and efficiency that other forms of marketing do not.

A newspaper, magazine, television, or radio news feature carries the implied endorsement of the media. This valuable endorsement cannot be purchased outright; it must be earned through newsworthiness. Once the news feature is obtained, reprints and tapes become potent and long-lived marketing tools. These can be used like brochures, only they are better than any printed material you could produce because they carry a third-party endorsement.

To calculate the relative value of a favorable article, we believe a good rule of thumb is to multiply the value of equivalent media space or time by three. In other words, if an advertisement of the same length or time would have cost $1,000 to purchase, then the relative value of that much publicity would be worth $3,000 if you had to purchase it.

Here's a for instance. Let's say, through your publicity genius, the *Morning Advocate* decided to write a story about your business. The story measured 100 column inches. The ad rate for a column inch in that newspaper is $32.34, so a 100-column inch display ad would cost you $3,234. But since this is publicity, we believe you would have to purchase three ads of that size to get the same marketing impact as the one news article.

Multiplying the relative space costs by three is used to account for the following:

1. implied endorsement of the media

2. increased readership or viewership over typical ads

3. premium positions not for sale ("You can't buy the front page.")

4. writer's fees, production, and typesetting costs borne by the media

We do not have a lot of hard data to back this up; it just makes sense. Look at the logic for each item. Item 1 examines the implied endorsement of the media. What do you believe more, an advertisement or a newspaper story? A commercial or a newscast? Dorothy Levy, in an article on the power of publicity over advertising in the *Public Relations Quarterly,* notes that "P.R. power is especially valuable when the public must not only know about a claim [which advertising can make known easily] but believe it." When morning drive-time personalities do ad-lib commercials for a sponsor versus a canned spot, there is always an extra charge. Radio stations believe this has more value, and they charge for it.

Item 2 looks at increased readership or viewership. What do you pay more attention to, the television program or the commercials? Don't you spend more time reading the newspaper articles than the ads? In 1985, advertising agency president David Oglivy pointed out that 85 percent of magazine readers do not read the body copy of advertisements, but they do read the articles.

Ad rates are based on the number of people that read, listen, or watch. Eric Bolland, who compared advertising and public relations in the *Public Relations Quarterly,* noted an important piece of research. A 1929 study by Starch, who conducted one of the earliest studies of advertising in publications, demonstrated that advertising readership is a function of position in a publication. Magazines charge extra for premium positions like the inside front cover. Radio stations charge extra for running the spot at a certain time, such as just prior to the morning business report.

Item 3 accounts for the fact that some things are not for sale at any price. You can't buy the *Mona Lisa.* You can't buy the Grand Canyon. You can't buy an ad on the front page of the *Wall Street Journal.* But *publicity* can get you there.

Item 4 is the least important, but it does add value. Writing, production, typesetting, photography, and other items are costs that the media pays for. However, publicity is not free. You have to write, produce, and photograph newsworthy items to get the attention of the media. Yet this does not cost as much as producing high-quality display ads and commercials. So with publicity, you come out ahead on the deal.

A basic principle of marketing is the AIDA formula: Awareness + Interest + Desire = Action. In order to get prospects to take the action you want, they must first become aware. Creating awareness is what publicity does best, but it has its drawbacks. You can't control the timing and the message like you can with advertising. But in the long run, nothing is more cost efficient at building awareness.

Publicity, as we stated, must be earned through its newsworthiness. In honor of P. T. Barnum, we present six publicity secrets that you can use to create news.

Secret One: The Publicity Stunt Lives

W. C. Fields once said, "Any man who hates kids and dogs can't be all bad." But when it comes to publicity stunts, you gotta love those kids, dogs, and every other animal. And publicists still enjoy the company of a good elephant.

Locals Take on Elephant at Area Restaurant

Who eats more salad—a 2,000-pound elephant or 20 hungry Tampa Bay residents?

Allie's, a new chain of restaurants from the Marriott Corporation, discovered the answer during the Great Elephant Challenge, a salad-eating competition at their restaurant at a Florida mall.

The event was the brainchild of Gary Bitner Public Relations. Since Allie's features a food bar with lots of salad, Lisa Warren of the Bitner agency thought a salad-eating contest was appropriate. She tied in charitable groups and a local radio station, Q-105, to ensure publicity success.

Two ten-person teams competed with Moxie the elephant for a $1,000 donation to charity. The two challenger teams were recruited by the Q-105 radio station disc jockeys and represented the Lowry Park Zoo and the Boys and Girls Club of Tampa. Moxie, a five-year-old African elephant, did her salad chomping for the American Cancer Society.

Each side had five minutes to chow down for charity. Elephants eat nearly 150 pounds of hay and drink about 40 gallons of water each day. Despite abstaining from salad dressing, Moxie was the winner. But the big winner was Allie's. Newspapers and television dutifully gave the event extensive pre- and post-event coverage.

Bless the Beasts and the Children

If you don't want to use an animal, consider what a child might be able to do. Here's an item from a 1990 Associated Press wire story.

```
       Disabled Stage Protest on Capitol Steps


    WASHINGTON (AP)—Using her arms to drag her
small body up the Capitol steps, eight-year-old
Jennifer Keelan yesterday joined some 60 disabled
Americans in lobbying for legislation to guarantee
their civil rights.

    I'll take all night if I have to," Jennifer
said to others crawling alongside her. She paused
just past the halfway point for a sip of water on
a bright and unreasonably hot March day.

    Keelan, a second-grader from Denver, was the
youngest of about 60 people with disabilities who
left their wheelchairs and crawled up the West
Front of the Capitol.

    They were making a symbolic protest to demand
passage of a key bill now pending in the House
that would extend civil rights to disabled
persons.


                    ###
```

Double Your Pleasure, Double Your Publicity

Creating a visual symbol, such as a salad-eating elephant or a small girl crawling up the Capitol steps, is the key to a good publicity stunt. And if one cute kid is good, Henry figured two must be better.

The challenge was to create news about the grand opening of a Doubletree Hotel. One hotel employee suggested the hotel cut a big ribbon with a big pair of scissors, an event unlikely to stop the presses in any town. Instead, Henry created the Doubletree Doubletake, a Hollywood casting call for identical twins and celebrity look-alikes.

Casting director Samuel Warren was hired to stage the event in the Doubletree parking lot one week prior to the grand opening. In addition to possible film work with Warren, casting call winners were promised appearances at a series of grand opening VIP parties.

One week before the hotel opened, the casting call was held in the parking lot. It was a chance for locals to be stars, and the event received extensive pre-publicity. More than 700 identical twins, mostly adorable children, and 50 celebrity look-alikes auditioned that day. Television news crews and newspaper photographers had a field day.

That week, hotel VIP party guests literally did a doubletake when they arrived at the hotel and were greeted by a long reception line of identical twins. Guests also got to pose for Polaroid photos with such star look-alikes as Clark Gable, Marilyn Monroe, Humphrey Bogart, Bill Cosby, Joan Collins, and Burt Reynolds.

Two sets of adult identical twins were hired for extra duty. They were dressed in hotel uniforms and delivered Doubletree's famous chocolate chip cookies on opening day to local reporters and editors. Even those media reps who didn't come to the casting call were doing a doubletake. It all helped add up to what one Doubletree executive termed "the most successful grand opening in the chain's history."

A No Bull Fight Against City Hall

You can't fight City Hall, but sometimes you can use it for some extra publicity. A little controversy can be newsworthy. Use this to your advantage when creating news. Some journalists think publicity stunts are a lot of bull. In Paul Tibolla's case, they'd be right. Tibolla is the owner of the Lotta-Bull restaurant in Rockville, Maryland, and he often roams around in a $300 bull suit drumming up business. "When I send the bull out, business goes up," he says.

He also received a $75 fine. The city's 1974 sign ordinance strictly forbids "free-standing signs which have the shape in the form of any person, animal, vegetable, product, or animation of any of the foregoing."

But can a sign walk? Tibolla argued it was a violation of his First Amendment rights. Taking the bull by the horns, he was willing to take the matter to the highest court in the land. The result was national publicity for his restaurant. His lawyer said that he "couldn't conceive how any jurisdiction could bust this bull."

Secret Two: And the Survey Said...

Another publicity secret is that the media loves numbers. An easy way to generate news that will get your name out there is to analyze and report statistics. Give the media provocative numbers, and they will give you coverage. This is what we term publicity-generating research.

This is how it works. Find a topic that relates to your organization. Commission an opinion survey. Then release the results to the media in a news release that offers your analysis.

When in Doubt, Blame the Television

Founded over a century ago to help families, the Independent Order of Foresters used publicity-generating research to gain its first national exposure.

The following news release, which resulted in coverage in such publications as *USA Today*, helped build awareness for the not-for-profit fraternal benefit society that serves families.

CONTACT: Henry DeVries (619) 755-5151

12/20/90

NEWS FROM

THE INDEPENDENT ORDER OF FORESTERS

PARENTS THINK THEY OUTSHINE THEIR PARENTS

SAN DIEGO—Sorry mom and dad. We're better parents, or at least we think we are.

Eighty percent of today's parents of school-age children say they are more effective than their parents, but admit their kids are helping less around the house and watching more television than they did as youngsters.

These issues surfaced in a recent national survey of 600 parents sponsored by the not-for-profit Independent Order of Foresters (IOF), one of the world's oldest and largest fraternal benefit societies.

The IOF is using the survey information to develop a series of free, effective parenting seminars across the country in 1990. Leading the seminars will be Dorothy and Robert DeBolt, whose efforts in raising 20 children have been featured in television specials and countless newspaper articles.

"Children are not being given the opportunity to contribute to family life, and television has become the great babysitter," says Robert DeBolt. "Many parents today are concentrating more on giving their kids material advantages and less on character building."

# # #

This news release was sent to 1,200 newspapers, radio stations, magazines, and television news shows through an electronic distribution service called PR Newswire at (800) 843-2495. For a few hundred dollars, this service or its competitor, BusinessWire at (800) 225-2030, gives the major American media the opportunity to see your news release on their computer screens.

Results can be impressive. For the IOF parenting survey, newspapers from the *Los Angeles Times* to the supermarket tabloid, the *Star*, reported the results of the study. Radio deejays and local TV news also carried the story. Six months after the release, many publications were still using the survey information in news stories.

Here are some other examples of publicity-generating research in action, all taken from *USA Today*.

- If you like steamy sex conversations over dinner, you're probably single, according to a survey of 300 men and women conducted by Sfuzzi, a trattoria with locations in New York; Washington, D.C.; Dallas; and Houston.

- One in three people suffer pangs of guilt along with pangs of hunger for a snack. The survey was conducted for Continental Baking Co., the maker of Twinkies, Hostess Cupcakes, and Ho Hos.

- The lowly penny has a big following with the public, says a Gallup poll. Of 750 adults asked if the penny should be discontinued, the con-cents-us was clear: 62 percent want to save the single-cent coin. The poll was commissioned by Americans of Common Cents, a group organized by the zinc industry. Pennies are made mostly of zinc and use less than 3 percent copper.

- A friendly, helpful staff is what 76 percent of patrons want at a fast-food restaurant, according to a Wendy's/Gallup survey of 1,029 fast-food consumers.

- People would rather pay $50 a month for insurance that includes a nursing home benefit than have free coverage without the benefit, says an American Association of Retired Persons study of 1,490 adults.

■   Cleveland and Nashville are among the ten cities that
will be hot for hotel development in 1990, say hotel real
estate consultants Laventhal & Horwath.

Here is another idea on how to distribute this information
nationally. News USA at (202) 393-2200 and the North American
Precis Syndicate at (818) 761-4012 are two of the nation's premier
newspaper feature placement services. These firms send monthly
packages of features to more than 10,000 daily and weekly
newspapers in the United States. You can expect 100 to 400
newspaper appearances per feature. For a fixed full-service fee,
News USA researches, writes, edits, typesets, prints, and
disseminates the material. Both provide physical clippings and
detailed usage reports.

Secret Three: Don't Buy When You Can Borrow

Can't afford to do a survey? No problem. There are plenty of free
numbers around.

Each month Chicago Title Company of San Diego issues an
analysis of new home sales. Finding the numbers costs nothing.
The data is pulled from county records and then organized in a
manner that can be easily understood. The local business pages
eagerly print the results.

The next page has an example of a typical news release.

CONTACT: Roni Hicks   (619) 238-8787

12/1/89

NEWS FROM

CHICAGO TITLE COMPANY

HOME SALES HIT THREE-YEAR LOW

SAN DIEGO—December 1989 was the lowest December in three years for home sales in San Diego County, an analysis by Chicago Title Company has found.

A total of 4,263 homes were sold during the month, compared to 6,788 in December 1988, a difference of 37 percent. In December 1987, 5,613 homes were sold, a difference of 24 percent compared to December 1989.

"The housing market has definitely cooled, and returned to moderate sales levels," said Jim Reiser, Chicago Title vice president and San Diego County branch manager.

# # #

The story continues for several paragraphs. Not only does the article build awareness for Chicago Title, it positions the company as the expert in its field.

Sometimes you have to get creative with this form of publicity. A transportation lobbying group released a study showing that traffic congestion costs the average motorist an estimated $1,200 a year in wasted time and gasoline. Instead of conducting a survey, the lobbyists calculated these figures using government highway statistics and current fuel prices.

The study was released by The Road Information Program (or TRIP, a handy acronym) to help increase coverage. The study showed that motorists could each spend as much as $5,200 in fuel and lost time by the year 2000 if the population continues to grow at its current pace. Another figure cited in the study was that more than 63 percent of the main roadways are in fair to poor condition.

Good analysis is essential in this type of publicity. "Traffic congestion is threatening to shut down the state's road and highway system," says Jack Maltester, president of Californians for Better Transportation, which commissioned the TRIP study. Another spokesperson called the wasted time and gas, "the congestion tax."

The group supported a victorious state constitutional amendment on the June 1990 ballot that raised state spending ceilings and increased the gasoline tax to pay for transportation improvements.

Another creative approach to playing with numbers was used by an environmental lobbying group from Washington, D.C. To gain coverage, a study should be provocative. Theirs was. In San Diego, the story appeared under the headline "High Levels of Lead Poisoning Suspected in San Diego Children."

More than 40 percent of young children in the city of San Diego may have levels of lead in their blood that could lower their IQ and cause behavior problems, reported a study by the Environmental Defense Fund.

More than 300 metropolitan areas were examined, thus giving the story national appeal and allowing the group to give each city a local angle. And where did they get the numbers? To arrive at these estimates, this 1990 study used data from a federal government health survey conducted from 1976 to 1980 and then projected lead exposure in children in various cities based primarily on the age of housing.

Although not based on actual measurements of kids in 300 towns, the figures proved to be within 5 percent of actual lead blood levels found in studies in Oakland and Baltimore.

Secret Four: If You're Desperate, Forget the Numbers

If you can't find the numbers you want, make a guess. And if you make it an educated guess, you still can get publicity. Next to numbers, the media like a bold analysis or prediction from an expert. Professional futurists, consultants who earn their living making forecasts based on current trends, are often quoted by the media. Consider the following:

- By the year 2008, the United States will have its first woman president. Voters of that day will have grown up with equal rights and women in politics.

- Soon the distinction between home and office will blur, thanks to a world of smart phones, fax machines, and computers.

- Meditation breaks will replace coffee breaks as older baby boomers keep working. Job changes will occur more often, and early retirement will vanish.

You, too, can be a futurist. Just stick to your area of expertise. Predicting the future makes great reading, and who's to say if you're wrong? Two examples of this type of publicity follow.

Women Warned of Workplace Hurdles

San Diego—There are still some hurdles that women must jump in order to compete in the workplace, a consultant maintains. Some feminine traits can sabotage women's careers, said Susan Griffin, executive director of Griffin and Wong, a training and education company.

"One specific tradition is being the support system," she said. "Women's primary roles are being a friend, mother and partner."

If a woman takes on the problems of other women, however, she is likely sabotaging her chances to advance, Griffin said.

The trait of being supportive isn't valued unless it's a human resource position where counseling is needed, she said. Male managers, she said, tend to frown on energy spent on caring for someone else's problems rather than getting work done.

According to Griffin, men and women also compete differently. Men take risks and admire each other. Women tend to want individual recognition—they're the only winner. (THE SAN DIEGO UNION)

Smith Sees GM's Share of Market Soaring to 60%

By: Rick Hagland

Newhouse News Service

(As it appeared in the
SAN DIEGO DAILY TRANSCRIPT)

DETROIT—Throughout his tumultuous reign as chairman of General Motors Corp., Roger Smith has said the payoff for the sweeping changes he has made won't be seen for years.

Now in his final months as chief executive of the world's largest automaker, Smith offers a seemingly improbable checklist of what he expects that payoff to be.

In a recent interview at GM headquarters in Detroit, Smith predicted that by the mid-1990s, GM's share of the U.S. car market will zoom to 40 percent from its current 35 percent.

He also said GM will have "an incredible run of products" in the early 1990s that will lead respected quality rankings like those of J.D. Power and Associates.

The Japanese, meanwhile, will see their U.S. market stall as GM and other domestic makers reach new heights of competitiveness, he said.

Secret Five: A Word of Advice about Consumer Tips

Would you like to make more money? Have a better sex life? Hang wallpaper without killing yourself? If you have the answers, or at least a few helpful hints, the media will be glad to share them with the world.

Consumer tips are one of the easiest forms of publicity to place in the media. Consider some of these examples.

- Confused about the nutrition information on food labels? The American Dietetic Association in Chicago offers the following tips on beating fat traps....(Associated Press)

- The Shell Motorist Club and the National Safety Association have put together a list of night-driving tips. We thought these were good reminders for all of us....*(Redbook)*

- Rub a candle on your window. Throw salt in the fireplace. Pencil your door. Put kitty litter under your car. A few simple tips can save home-owners thousands of dollars, according to the Fieldstone Company, recently named "1990 Builder of the Year" by *Professional Builder* magazine....*(San Francisco Examiner Chronicle)*

- A recent survey of 600 United States parents conducted by the Independent Order of Foresters revealed that their first concern is their children's self-esteem. We all want our children to lead happy and productive lives, and a good self image plays an important role. Here are some well-tested approaches, offered by experts in the field of parent education....*(Indiana City Press)*

Here is a proven method for developing the advice that you need.

1. Pretend a reporter is interviewing you for this story. What wisdom would you be sure to include? Write it *all* down.

2. After you have brainstormed the list, cut it down to your five to twelve best points.

3. Write these up as your industry insider consumer tips, adding a few words of analysis attributed to your organization's spokesperson.

Vagabond Inns, a chain of approximately forty motels in the Western United States, used this strategy to gain national publicity for its twenty-fifth anniversary.

Top executives were polled on what secrets they would share with a relative or a close friend about staying in hotels. The answers were pulled together in a study called the "Vagabond Inns Insider Report." Several magazines and a wire service columnist published the information and quoted the hotel chain's president as the information source.

This exposure was then parlayed into radio and television interviews. An attractive spokesperson purchased several of the latest travel gadgets so she would have something visual to talk about. A television interview show was so impressed that they taped a series of three- to five-minute travel tip fillers, which they aired and credited to Vagabond Inns for a whole year. Other than the travel gadgets and a little time, the cost of this publicity was minimal.

Want an excuse to go bananas around the house? Coauthor Diane came up with several when she was researching how to publicize a Caribbean restaurant that seemingly uses them in everything from appetizers to entrees to desserts. Several feature stories on the restaurant resulted from a simple news release on different ways to use this appealing fruit.

Secret Six: A Winner of an Idea for Publicity

A really good idea for publicity is a really bad contest. The undisputed champion in this category for more than a decade promised that "one really good page of really bad Hemingway could land you and a friend in Italy."

Harry's Bar & American Grill used an International Imitation Hemingway Competition for more than ten years to promote its restaurants in Los Angeles and San Francisco. Announced annually with modest posters and news releases, the contest attracted more than 20,000 entries from around the world since its inception in 1977. Extensive coverage of the call for entries and the results would be generated by news releases such as the following:

CONTACT: Mark Grody (213) 479-3363

1/10/88

NEWS FROM

HARRY'S BAR & AMERICAN GRILL

ANNUAL INTERNATIONAL HEMINGWAY COMPETITION SEEKS ENTRIES

The prizes are Fame, Immortality and some nice food in Florence, Italy. But first, you must face the White Bull that is Paper With No Words On It.

You have done an Imitation Hemingway before, yes?

Don't look at your feet. We have all done it. A character sketch, some dialogue, maybe a love letter, no?

Write one page of Imitation Hemingway. It must mention Harry's Bar, nicely. It must sound like Hemingway, read like Hemingway and it must be funny. (The winner will be very funny.)

Now is the moment of truth.

It is raining and that is good because without rain there would be no writing. You should sit at an outside table in the sun and talk and laugh and feed the little birds.

(more)

HARRY'S BAR & GRILL
ADD ONE

But the tables have been taken inside. The little birds are gone, and so is the sun.

Across the prizes and into the rules. The winner wins dinner for two at Harry's Bar & American Grill in Florence, Italy. We fly the two of you there. We fly you back. Finito. Entries must be postmarked by February 15, 1988. The decision of the judges will be final. All entries become the property of Harry's Bar & American Grill.

# # #

The Yellow Roach of Texas

First runner-up goes to the Bizzy Bees Pest Control Company. Using a poster worthy of the Texas Rangers, Bizzy Bees owner Michael Bohdan offered a $1,000 reward for the largest cockroach in Dallas—Wanted Dead or Alive. Dead was preferable.

Even *People* magazine devoted a full page to the winning 1.9-inch fallen hero of the Lone Star state. This critter was gunned down with bug spray while running away from three women who work for the local phone company. He posthumously won out over 14 finalists, 9 of them dead, who had been selected from a field of 204.

The Best of the Worst

Third place in this category goes to a prized effort that promotes a West Coast university. Here is a story from United Press International about the annual event.

Passion for Purple Prose
Produces Perverse Prize

SAN JOSE (UPI)—With ease, Linda Vernon penned the worst piece of writing among 10,000 entries worldwide in the annual Bulwer-Lytton Fiction Contest.

Vernon, 38, a homemaker and mother of three from Newark, in Alameda County, entered the contest while taking an adult education night class in creative writing at Ohlone College. She'll receive a word processor and a "handsome simulated parchment certificate." Her winning entry:

"Dolores breezed along the surface of her life like a flat stone forever skipping along smooth water, rippling reality sporadically but oblivious to it consistently, until she finally lost momentum, sank and, due to an overdose of fluoride as a child which caused her to suffer from chronic apathy, doomed herself to lie forever on the floor of her life as useless as an appendix and as lonely as a 500-pound barbell in a steroid-free fitness center."

Contest entrants compose bad opening sentences to imaginary novels in the international contest sponsored by San Jose State University. It celebrates English author Edward Bulwer-Lytton, who first penned the phrase, "It was a dark and stormy night." Another winning entry:

Kenneth Leffler, law student from Falls Church, Va., top historical award: "Paul von Hindenburg, only one month old and wrapped in a blue blanket, rested peacefully in his cradle, oblivious to the tragedy that would one day befall a dirigible to be named after him."

# # #

Contest publicity abounds. For a minimal investment, even a small business can generate national coverage. Here are some honorable mention examples to inspire you to enter this field of endeavor.

- A small bed and breakfast inn in New England received national coverage, including a story in *USA Today*, about its recipe contest to find the nation's best chocolate chip cookie to serve each night to guests.

- A California car care products company captured the attention of almost every drive-time radio personality with its search for the American who commutes the farthest distance to work each day. The winner: a 408-mile-per-day New York City-to- Connecticut roundtripper.

- For more than thirty years the ultimate in cooking is the Pillsbury Bake-Off, which now offers more than $120,000 in prizes. But when you consider all the publicity Pillsbury gets, it is definitely worth the dough.

NEWS RELEASE

Contact: Sally Romoser or Susan Reed
(619) 238-8787

9/21/89

NEWS FROM
RONI HICKS & ASSOCIATES, INC.

THE INDEPENDENT ORDER OF FORESTERS SELECTS RONI HICKS & ASSOCIATES FOR PUBLIC RELATIONS

Roni Hicks & Associates has been named by the Independent Order of Foresters (IOF) to handle its national public relations, announced Roni Hicks, president of the full-service advertising and public relations agency.

The IOF, one of the world's oldest and largest family fraternal benefit societies, is a nonprofit, nondenominational group that actively participates in various charitable projects in their communities. Founded in 1874 in Newark, New Jersey, the IOF, which has headquarters in Solana Beach, California, Canada, and the United Kingdom, comprises more than one million members in those countries.

Roni Hicks & Associates will design and implement a campaign to raise community awareness of the IOF's child abuse prevention and good parenting programs.

(more)

IOF FORESTERS
ADD ONE

"The Independent Order of Foresters is an exemplary organization," Hicks said, "This will be a most interesting and rewarding account for us."

In addition to Hicks, other members of the IOF account team are Henry DeVries, executive vice president and Jennifer Wilson, account executive/
public relations.

Celebrating its 10th anniversary in 1989, Roni Hicks & Associates provides marketing, advertising, and public relations counsel to clients in real estate, health care, and entertainment industries.

###

SC/tw

NEWS RELEASE

Contact: Rick Griffin, (619) 296-8806

12/21/87

NEWS FROM
DR. STEVEN PETERSON

SAN DIEGANS ARE LOOKING BETTER
THANKS TO ORTHOKERATOLOGY

Like braces are used for crooked teeth, a San Diego eye doctor is using contact lenses for correcting myopia vision problems.

(more)

DR. PETERSON
ADD ONE

Dr. Steven Peterson, for the past five years, has cared for several thousand patients who have enjoyed improved vision thanks to a new, nonsurgical procedure called orthokeratology, which treats myopia, or nearsightedness, by altering the curvature of the cornea with the use of contact lenses.

Myopia, or nearsightedness, is when a person can't clearly see objects at a distance.

Dr. Peterson's mentor, Dr. Charles May, pioneered orthokeratology 25 years ago and has helped more than 10,000 people to see better. Dr. May recently retired.

"Sight is our principal means of interpreting and enjoying the world around us," said Dr. Peterson. But, if we're nearsighted, distant objects appear out of focus or totally unrecognizable. In a few months, orthokeratology can rectify a person's vision problems for a lifetime. It's not necessary to live today with blurred vision."

Orthokeratology uses contact lenses to change the curvature of the cornea to a more spherical shape, so that light will be focused directly on the retina, instead of in front of the retina, which is the case with myopia.

(more)

DR. PETERSON
ADD TWO

Every six to eight weeks, a person with imperfect vision is fitted with a new hard contact lens, which will result in gradually reshaping and improving the curvature of the cornea. These gradual changes can be observed scientifically.

With each new contact lens prescription, the new lenses, with less curvature and less myopia correction, will meet the new needs of the eye as it progresses toward more perfect vision.

"Orthokeratology is a safe and proven method for treating and reducing nearsightedness," said Dr. Peterson. "Today, people can have perfect vision restored."

###

RG/sr

NEWS RELEASE

Contact: Sally Romoser or Susan Reed
         (619) 238-8787

12/28/89

NEWS FROM
RONI HICKS & ASSOCIATES, INC.

RONI HICKS & ASSOCIATES WINS
THREE NATIONAL MERCURY AWARDS

SAN DIEGO—Images of an elegant Italian era and a campaign for a local bank using famous international personalities received national honors for Roni Hicks & Associates at the third

annual Mercury Awards, held Dec. 6 at the Sheraton Centre Hotel in New York City.

The full-service marketing, advertising, and public relations firm won a gold award for financial media relations and letterhead designs, according to Roni Hicks, president.

Sponsored by the National Media Conference, the Mercury Awards honors outstanding achievement in communications and public relations. More than 900 entries from firms nationwide were received for the competition.

The gold award cited the firm's campaign for the Bank of San Diego. One silver award lauded the agency's corporate advertisement for the Italian-themed master-planned community of Renaissance-La Jolla and another silver award cited the stationery design for the townhouse community of Avanti at Renaissance-La Jolla.

(more)

HICKS AWARDS
ADD ONE

The gold award recognizes work in the nation's top 95th percentile, and the silver acknowledges work in the top 85th percentile. More than 250 individual judges from 20 firms nationwide reviewed award entries, each of which was judged three times.

Celebrating its 10th anniversary in 1989, Roni Hicks & Associates provides marketing, advertising, and public relations services to clients in the real estate, health care, and hospitality industries.

SC/tjm

NEWS RELEASE

Contact: Steve Carpowich or Susan Reed
       (619) 238-8787

12/21/89

NEWS FROM
ARCHITECTS LORIMER-CASE

ARCHITECTS LORIMER-CASE TO DESIGN CHURCH OF ST. LUKE IN RANCHO SAN DIEGO

The award-winning firm of Architects Lorimer-Case has been named to design the Church of St. Luke in Rancho San Diego, announced David Lorimer, principal for Lorimer-Case.

The Catholic church, which will cover 20,000 square feet, will be designed in a style reminiscent of classic California missions. The design will utilize a cloistered arrangement,

(more)

LORIMER-CASE
ADD ONE

comprising a group of interconnected buildings surrounding a courtyard area. The buildings will house the church, classrooms, and office spaces.

"Lorimer-Case has come up with a grand plan," said Church of St. Luke Pastor Raymond Gerard O'Donnell. "Our parishioners will be very pleased with their new home."

The church has recently completed two pledge drives for its building fund and plans to continue a concerted fund-raising effort. No groundbreaking date has yet been set.

Founded in 1974, the award-winning firm of Architects Lorimer-Case has designed single-family and multi-family homes, hotels, office buildings, mixed-use commercial complexes, and historical renovations.

SC/tw

NEWS RELEASE

Contact: Rick Griffin or Susan Reed
(619) 296-8806

6/9/88

NEWS FROM
CHICAGO TITLE CO.

SINGLE-FAMILY HOMES MORE POPULAR THAN CONDOS IN FIRST QUARTER OF '88, SAYS CHICAGO TITLE

San Diego-based builders in the first quarter of this year made plans to build nearly 1,000 single-family, detached homes than condominium homes and attached townhomes, according to a just-released report by Chicago Title, one of San Diego's largest title insurance companies.

"Single-family, detached housing is still more popular than condos or townhomes in San Diego County," said Denis V. Rottler, Chicago Title vice president and San Diego County manager, "Because mortgage interest rates have remained low, builders are a little less hesitant than in previous months. We're expecting a healthy local building season this spring."

According to Chicago Title, from January to March of this year, maps were filed with the county recorder's office for 56 subdivision tracks, representing 2,687 single-family, detached homes, and 65 condominium and townhome tracks, representing 1,717 units.

The first quarter of 1988 compares to the first quarter of previous years in the following ways:—The number of single-family homes planned in the first quarter of 1988 is more than any

(more)

CHICAGO TITLE
ADD ONE

first quarter in the previous six years, and 37 percent higher than the first quarter of 1987.

"We're noticing tremendous growth potential in the 'move-up market,'" said Rottler, referring to existing home owners who have enough savings and equity in their current home to afford a bigger, better, brand-new detached home.

—The number of condos and townhomes planned in the first quarter of 1988 is only 5 percent more than the units planned in the first quarter of 1987. During the first quarter of the past seven years, 1985 was the best for condo construction with 2,555 units planned.

"The condo market appears stable because condos are sometimes more affordable than many single-family homes, especially for first-time buyers," Rottler said.

—Fewer single-family subdivision tracks were planned in the first quarter of 1988, compared to the first quarters of 1982 through 1986.

"Building limitations placed by local governments on builders throughout San Diego County, I believe, are moderately slowing down some development. But it's impossible to force builders to cease building, especially when there's such a public demand for new housing," said Rottler.

Chicago Title Co., originally founded in 1885, is one of San Diego County's largest title

(more)

CHICAGE TITLE
ADD TWO

insurance companies both in market share and premium revenue. In 1986, in the largest merger of its kind in the history of the title insurance industry, Chicago Title Co. joined forces with Safeco Title Insurance Co. This created the nations's largest family of title insurance underwriters with more than 5,000 locations. Chicago Title's local operations are headquartered at 1301 Third Avenue in downtown San Diego,

###

RG/tjm

QUERY LETTER

January 31, 1990

Ms. Joan Thursh
Articles Editor
Good Housekeeping
959 Eighth Avenue
New York, NY 10019

Dear Ms. Thursh:

Prevention is the best medicine when it comes to health care for your house.

Regular check-ups and some simple treatment can save home owners thousands of dollars. Dave Dennig, construction specialist for the 1990 Home Builder of the Year, can't make house calls but does have a bag of wellness tips to share.

Most sound like quirky home remedies or good luck tricks from the witch doctor:

- Rub candles on windows
- Throw salt in the fireplace
- Pencil your doors
- Put kitty litter under your car

Each is designed to ward against premature aging. Rubbing candle wax along window tracks for lubrication is gentler to nylon rollers and won't attract dust like oil. Adding salt to the fireplace helps prevent soot build-up while adding color to the flame.

With figures from the National Association of Realtors showing that the average home owner stays in one residence for seven years, long-term care is a must.

"Regular maintenance is the key to protecting most people's biggest investment, their home," says Dennig of the Fieldstone Co., a Southern California firm named 1990 Builder of the Year by *Professional Builder* magazine.

He can share his 23 tips and other advice for your readers who want to nurse their home back to health.

I will call in a few days for some exploratory surgery on this idea.

Sincerely,
Roni Hicks & Associates, Inc.

Henry J. DeVries
Executive Vice President

HJD/tjm

P.S. Dennig estimates the cost for maintaining a home is $120 a year. Compare that to $2,500 to implant a new tub damaged by poor grouting care.

ARTICLE PROPOSAL

Tips for Finding an Expert Witness

Looking for an expert witness? Here are likely places to find them:

1. Reputed businesses in the field, such as Big Eight or local accounting and consulting firms

2. Other attorneys who have used expert witnesses

3. Opposing experts on previous cases your attorney has handled

4. Professional associations, such as the local bar association

5. Expert witness registries, such as the Technical Advisory Service for Attorneys (TASA), 800-523-2319

6. Expert witness directories in particular fields

7. Professors at colleges and universities

8. Forensic Consultants Association, Bill Scudder, President, call Lynday Laws at 619-481-1990

9. National Consultant Referrals, Inc., 1-800-221-3104 or 619-552-0111

10. Industry trade groups

What was a fair and reasonable measure of damages suffered by a commercial developer who bought property unaware it was in a flood zone? Tamra Tilton, C.P.A., a partner in Streamline Financial and Productivity Consultants in San Diego and Phoenix, was called upon by Attorney Paul S. Rowley, J.D., to serve as a financial expert witness.

Her role was to evaluate the plaintiff's claim of damages to see if it was reasonable, sound, and accurate. As a result of her analysis, Tilton disagreed with the plaintiff's's claim by a difference of over $1 million.

Did a developer create an unsafe roadway that caused a car to hydroplane and crash? Larry Louns, J.D., a partner in the litigation department of Luce, Forward, Hamilton, and Scripps, hired a meteorologist, hydrologist, and civil engineer as expert witnesses. Their charge was to analyze the amount of rain, runoff, and absorption capability of the soil surrounding the road to determine if the developer was at fault.

What is the appropriate use of restraints on adolescents in juvenile hall? Charles Ettari, M.D., a psychiatrist in private practice in La Jolla, will testify in a class action suit in Orange County after evaluating the institution's policy, procedures, and incident reports.

Besides strengthening legal cases, testifying as an expert witness strengthens the bottom line of a forensic specialist. In fact, some leave jobs in their chosen professions to become fulltime expert witnesses. Although, ironically, most attorneys still prefer to hire experts who are not fulltime witnesses.

"When cross-examining an expert on the witness stand, the opposing attorney will use every weapon at his disposal in an attempt to discredit," says Tilton. "For this reason, continuing to practice in your field has a decided advantage." Tilton has combined litigation and financial and management consulting into her business, which recently opened an office in San Diego, after launching two years ago in Phoenix.

PAGE 3

Engineer John Fiske Brown of Solana Beach has built a 10-person firm which solely performs forensic engineering. "During a deposition or on the witness stand, you can't rely on books or references," he says. "You sink or swim based on your knowledge."

"Many clients demand that expert witnesses testify in their cases because they believe their chances of winning a case will improve if the judge and jury can hear the facts from a nonbiased third party," says Tilton. "And while expert witnesses aren't inexpensive, hiring them is more cost-effective than an attorney's taking a crash course in cost-accounting or metallurgy."

Ettari concurs. "Decisions made within the legal process are far reaching. By hiring a specialist to study the evidence and give an expert opinion, you give the judge and jury more and better information on which to base their judgment."

###

NEWS RELEASE

Contact: Rick Griffin or Susan Reed
(619) 296-8806

5/26/88

NEWS FROM
CHICAGO TITLE CO.

CHICAGO TITLE SPONSORS LENDER'S FAIR JUNE 3

Chicago Title Co., one of San Diego's largest title insurance companies, is sponsoring the fifth annual Lender's Fair on Friday, June 3, from 9 a.m. to 5 p.m. at the Town and Country Hotel Convention Center in Mission Valley.

More than 3,000 real estate agents from throughout San Diego County are expected to attend the annual day-long real estate trade exposition.

The program will include six real estate experts discussing the latest trends affecting the industry, and exhibits from 80 lending institutions, each offering information on the latest loan programs available.

Cost is $2 per person in advance, and $3 the day of the event. Tickets are available from Chicago Title representatives or call Jim Reiser at Chicago Title at (619) 235-7202.

The program will include the following speakers:

* At 9:30 a.m., Don Bauder, financial editor of the San Diego Union, on San Diego's economic outlook;

(more)

LENDER'S FAIR
ADD ONE

* At 10:30 a.m., H. Wayne Perry, President of
  Ameristar Financial, on the future of mortgage
  banking;

* At 11:30 a.m., Joseph E. La Liberte from
  RNG Mortgage, on the latest in VA and FHA
  financing;

* At 1:30 a.m., Stephen Coury, of the Building
  Industry Association, on the current growth/no
  growth debate

* At 2:30 p.m., George Kramer, President of Cal
  Coast, on adjustable rate mortgages, and

* At 3:30 p.m., Mike Ferry, of Mike Ferry
  Productions, on sales motivation.

Chicago Title Co., originally founded in 1885,
is one of Southern California's largest title
insurance companies both in market share and
premium revenue. In 1986, in the largest merger
of its kind in the history of the title insurance
industry, Chicago Title Co. joined forces with
Safeco Title Insurance Co. The merger created the
nation's largest family of title insurance
underwriters with more than 5,000 locations.

In San Diego, Chicago Title's operations are
headquartered at 1301 Third Ave. in downtown San
Diego.

RG/mk

QUERY LETTER

8885 Rio San Diego Dr., Suite 335
San Diego, California 92108
Phone # (619) 297-2400
Fax # (619) 297-2588

May 17, 1990

Gayle Falkenthal
Producer
KSDO Radio
5050 Murphy Canyon Road
San Diego, CA 92123

Dear Gayle:

Is women's solidarity a form of reverse discrimination?

Today in the United States there are 20 "Women's Directories" published for women by women in cities such as Philadelphia, Los Angeles, Chicago, and Denver. The purpose of these directories is to provide a listing of women-owned businesses for the community's women to patronize and support.

San Diego's own fledgling Women's Directory is gaining a strong foothold in its second year, garnering advertising support from established women-owned businesses and new ones alike.

The wave of women supporting the growth and success of other women has been cresting with events such as last February's second annual "Regional Conference for Women" and the upcoming "Wonder Women 2000, A Celebration of Women in Business" to be held on 3 to 9 p.m., Tuesday, June 5, 1990 at the Town & Country Convention Center.

While the tide of sisterhood is rising, and not just among what some people consider staunch

PAGE 2

feminists, some in San Diego's male population can be heard grumbling under their breath. The main complaint centers around the fact that men would never be able to "get away with" a directory of men-owned businesses or a symposium for men.

Are publications such as the women's directory and events such as "Wonder Women 2000" a form of reverse discrimination or are they long-overdue recognition and support for a segment of the working population that has been maligned and taken advantage of?

Mary Ellen Hamilton, publisher of the San Diego Women's Directory and cosponsor of "Wonder Women 2000" would like to discuss this issue on Roger's show and is willing to answer callers' questions on this controversial issue.

Gayle, I will call you to discuss this angle. If it does not appeal to you, we have several other ideas.

Best regards,

Deborah Purdy
The Gage Group

Top Self-Marketing Secrets

Six Publicity Secrets

1. Publicity stunts still work wonders. For best results, try to tie in a visual symbol such as a child or an animal.

2. The media love to report numbers, so pick a provocative topic that relates to your position and commission a publicity-generating survey.

3. If you don't have the budget to commission a survey, find some numbers to analyze that relate to your positioning. Quote yourself extensively providing expert analysis.

4. Make an educated prediction or analysis. If you provide a solid analysis, you will get publicity.

5. Research industry insider tips that you can pass along to consumers. The media welcome helpful advice and view it as a public service.

6. Contests are a winning idea for publicity. The best publicized contests contain an element of humor and the media can use them to add entertainment value to the news.

7

You Don't Have to Be a Writer to Get Published
Ghost Writers in Disguise

Do all of the articles in publications that are read by your peers and prospects seem to carry the bylines of your competitors? How do those people set themselves up as author experts? What does it take to get published? And if you don't have the time or the experience to write yourself, how do you find a collaborator or ghost writer?

Authoring articles to become a quoted authority is a time-tested vehicle for gaining credibility in a specific area. Professors do it to win tenure; physicians do it to earn recognition and top positions; and businesspeople do it to set themselves up as experts in their fields. Others write to establish that they were the first to coin a phrase or to solve a problem in a certain way.

It's not just getting the byline that turns sales. It's learning how to merchandise your writing that makes the difference between an article that is caught between the covers of a trade journal and one that goes to work to bring in new prospects. Once you learn how to market yourself to an editor to get a writing assignment, it's essential to learn how to subtly wave the bylined piece in front of those who need to see it.

Sell Angles, Not Credentials

Everyone who writes a magazine article or book was not born with a silver pen in hand. Don't let the fact that you sweat over having to write a two-paragraph letter keep you from tackling a 1,500-word article or a ten-chapter book. The ability to write is about fourth on the list of what it takes to sell your writing. The ability to spot a salable angle, professionalism, and unwavering persistence are more important than writing talent.

Finding a topic that is timely, noteworthy, and not overdone is the most crucial element of scoring a byline. But just touting a topic for discussion is not enough. Add an intriguing spin on a certain aspect of that topic to prove to the editor or publisher that you have something to say (that boldly goes where no writer has gone before).

This is the elusive angle on an idea that good writers spend their lives stalking. While editors say there are no good ideas left—they've covered them all—they bend over backwards to find new angles on old ideas that their competitors have yet to spot. And if you're the one who can feed them that angle—regardless of your ability to write—you will earn the ear of the editor and either a byline or an attribution in the publication.

To find an angle, take your topic and look at it from every possible perspective. Break down the idea into as many different pieces as you can. Then ask yourself what you know about each piece that may be different from what others know or have heard.

Here's a list of bland ideas that will make an editor of a targeted publication yawn as he or she tosses the article proposal into the wastebasket, and a corresponding list of tantalizing angles that shout "new and intriguing." The business trying to market the idea is also listed so that you get a sense of who's selling what ideas and why.

Business:	Canned tuna company
Target:	National health magazine
Self-serving Idea:	Our tuna is high in Omega 3, which has been touted as a health benefit.
Angle Sold:	How the canning process affects the Omega 3 in canned tuna.

Business: Women's directory
Target: Local business magazine
Self-serving Idea: We're holding a symposium filled with
                     interesting workshops. One is on stress
                     management.
Angle Sold: How top executives are using meditation to
                     combat stress.

Business: Plastic surgeon
Target: National Women's Magazine
Self-serving Idea: I use tissue expansion to help overcome
                     the negatives of skin grafts.
Angle Sold: Plastic surgeon repairs the face of a
                     five-year-old girl using state-of-the-art
                     tissue expansion techniques.

Business: Human resource training group
Target: In-flight magazine
Self-serving Idea: We teach two-way communication in
                     our seminars.
Angle Sold: Overcoming twelve communication road-
                     blocks through active listening.

Business: Psychologist
Target: National Teen Magazine
Self-serving Idea: I help teens and parents work through
                     problems.
Angle Sold: How not to pick up your parents' bad
                     habits.

If a fresh slant for your idea doesn't come to mind, dream up a magazine article or book title for your idea to help you focus on what is unique. Be clever in creating titles—use plays on words, rework tired clichés, and use the rhythm and rhyme of songs to get you thinking. Often it's the title that sells a magazine article or book, so coming up with the title first can help you zero in on the angle.

A good title will go a long way toward selling your book or article. *Smart Women, Foolish Choices; How to Swim with the Sharks Without Being Eaten Alive;* and *The One-Minute Manager* all build intrigue into their titles and get their angles out front and in the open.

Take a look at this list of great magazine titles and see if they don't make you want to read on.

- Don't Be a One-Man Band (*Nation's Business*)
- Little Grown-ups: Why Some Kids Are Too Mature for Their Own Good (*Working Mother*)
- Calling in the Caterer: Leaving the Party to the Pros (*San Diego Magazine*)
- Terms of Engagement: The Fun and Formalities (*Bridal Guide*)
- Upstaging Time (*Lear's*)
- So Who Wants to Play Fair? (*Venture*)
- How to Sell Your Ideas (and Silence Your Critics) (*Working Woman*)
- Check Mates: Joint Accounts or Separate Ones, Almost All Couples Keep Some Money Secret (*Self*)
- Secrets of Winning on Wall Street (*Sylvia Porter's Personal Finance*)
- The Party's Over: Women Who Love Alcoholic Men (*New Woman*)

How to Pitch Your Magazine or Trade Journal Idea

Once you've honed your angle, you're ready to approach an editor. Don't pick up the phone and call. Just as if you were selling any other product, you need to write a convincing, professional proposal. But don't worry, it doesn't need to be lengthy; in fact, the shorter the better.

Editors want ideas submitted in the form of a one-page letter called a query. They don't want to see the entire manuscript. And you're wasting your time by writing the entire article before you know if you have a salable idea or the specific slant an editor may want.

Query letters do three primary things. They

1. Demonstrate that you have a fresh angle on an important topic.

2. Show that you have the ability to write the article in a way that will interest the magazine's readers.

3. Prove that you are the expert to write it.

It's important that your letter not just whisper your idea in a boring business letter style. It must trumpet it in a way that will be music to the ears of an editor whose in-basket is deluged with proposals from professional writers, public relations agencies, and others who want to see their name in print. Your first paragraph—the lead to your letter—should capture the imagination of the editor by painting a scenario with a real-life anecdote, offering a startling statistic, posing an intriguing question, or turning a phrase in such a way that it makes the editor want to know more.

Read the following leads from a few queries we've written to see how the introductory paragraph in a query differs significantly from the first paragraph of a traditional business letter.

(To USAir)
Nearly every American boy dreams of playing baseball in the major leagues. Stepping up to the plate on a warm summer day and cracking one over the center field wall to the roar of the crowd is a romantic, but rarely realized, fantasy. But for a few days a year, the dream comes alive for men who enroll in what has become known as fantasy baseball camp.

(To *Nation's Business*)
"A leader isn't worth much if he can't step in and take charge." "If you want something done right, you've got to do it yourself." "Good managers have all the answers."

Such take-charge sentiments are natural for company leaders. Since owners or managers of small and medium-sized companies are ultimately responsible for the success of their businesses, they feel compelled to perform or oversee every aspect of their operations.

(To *Modern Maturity*)
When your sleepy-eyed grandchild says, "Tell me a story," do you reach for a book to read instead of stretching your imagination?

"I'm no storyteller," you may think, remembering that your own dad seemed to have a special knack for telling tales. But we're all storytellers. What did you do the last time you explained to someone why you were late?

(To *American Way*)
Jim stormed out of the department meeting disgusted with the resistance to his ideas for boosting sales in a sagging account. "What's the use of coming up with innovative ideas around here?" he scowled. If you were Jim's boss how would you respond? a) "Don't worry, you'll come up with another good campaign." b) "I understand, I have trouble getting new ideas across myself." c) "Sounds like you're discouraged about trying to change things." d) "Can't you rethink key aspects of the campaign and present it again next week?"

Once you've introduced your topic with intrigue, tell the editor the proposed title of your article or book; then summarize the main points that you'll cover. If you plan to quote other experts in the field, share a name or two from your source file with the editor. Then let the editor know why his or her readers will be interested in this topic and why it's timely. Finally, end the query by giving a small sampling of your background in the field. If you've had other articles with your byline published, paper clip two or three examples to the proposal, attach a self-addressed, stamped envelope for a reply, and tuck it all into a nine-by-twelve-inch envelope to drop in the mail.

Although the process is time-consuming and seems archaic, most editors request that you do not send the same query letter to a number of magazines simultaneously. They want the first right to see an idea and to not have to worry that if they invest the time to evaluate your query letter and decide to buy it, that other editors may also be making the same decision. While the natural business inclination is to want to get a number of requests and to sell to the highest bidder, turning down an editor's offer because you have gotten a better deal from another publication is the fastest way to destroy a relationship with a magazine.

Unless your idea is extremely timely, wait four to six weeks to follow up with the editor to whom you've sent your query, either by a phone call or by sending a note with a copy of the original query. If the first editor isn't interested, send a newly printed copy of your query to another magazine. Don't let one rejection slip discourage you. If the editor has taken the time to say why the idea won't work, evaluate the opinion to determine if you need to do more work on the query. If you don't see the need to revise the query, mail it out again. Coauthor Diane once had a query on a timely topic rejected by six major women's magazines, but the seventh was a charm. The article sold on its seventh try to *McCall's* for a fee of $3,000.

We said don't call in your ideas, but there's always someone who breaks the rule and wins. When Arnold Rincover, Ph.D., a child psychologist and an award-winning, best-selling author, wanted to change careers from a university researcher to author, he called the major newspaper in his area, the *Toronto Star* and asked if they would be interested in a psychology column. Likewise, he called a prominent agent and expressed his interest in writing a book on child rearing.

"To my utter shock, both said 'yes,'" says Rincover. "My columns—which to that point had never been written—began selling for $200 a month and my book, which took a year to write, sold to Random House Canada and later in the United States to Simon and Schuster Pocket Books Division."

Later to expand his income, Rincover once again picked up the phone and called newspapers around the country to try to syndicate his column. "I sent samples, followed up with calls and more calls until they gave me a definite yes or no. Some took it, some didn't, but many major newspapers said yes. In fact, one editor said he wasn't interested in the column on psychology but asked if I knew someone who could write one on parenting. I said, 'Yes, me.' I went back to the other papers that turned down the first column and offered the second, and many bought it. I was now reaching millions of people, getting paid thousands of dollars, and just writing two columns."

Identifying Your Magazine Market

Knowing who to send your magazine queries to for maximum return takes more than cruising by the supermarket newsstand and picking out your favorite business magazine. It may be easy to spot *Inc.* or *Forbes* on the rack, but hundreds of other writers are submitting ideas to those publications every day. In addition to the obvious consumer magazines, whose addresses you can find in *Writer's Market* (a compendium of magazines and of publishing houses), don't overlook trade journals.

These specialty magazines are written for very specific audiences, and there is a trade journal for virtually every vocation and avocation. You'll target your public better through trade journals, since primarily human resource personnel read *Human Resource Executive;* only firefighters and paramedics spend time poring over *Emergency* magazine; and it's usually construction managers who digest the pages of *Building Design & Construction* with their morning coffee.

Although trade journal editors traditionally have smaller staffs than large consumer magazines, they receive fewer unsolicited ideas from writers and are more likely to give you a chance. And, even if your writing doesn't rival that of Tom Clancy, the editor may sense your expertise and be willing to edit your work or assign a ghost writer to assist you.

You'll find a good sampling of the names and addresses of trade journals in *Writer's Market,* but more exhaustive listings are included in *Standard Rate and Data, Bacon's Publicity Checker, Ulrich's International Periodical Directory, Seriel's Directory*, and *Association Periodicals* (published by the Encyclopedia of Association).

What It Takes to Sell a Book

Authoring a book is the ultimate way to prove that you have a lot to say on a subject. If your book is published, it immediately serves as a third-party endorsement for your credibility, since the publisher was obviously impressed enough by your expertise to sign you.

Once again, a proposal is your sales call to a publisher. You can read entire books on the subject. (One that we recommend is *How to Write a Book Proposal* by Michael Larsen, Writer's Digest Books, 1985.) Here are the basics to determine if this is an avenue you'll want to pursue. Before you put pen to paper, it's essential to do a cursory literary search to determine what else has been written on your subject and if your book will significantly differ from the competition. This will let you identify your niche in the book marketplace, and you'll use this information when you write a marketing statement for the publisher.

Next, be sure that you have enough to say on the topic. A common reason that editors turn down book ideas is because they are not pithy enough to warrant 250 to 350 manuscript pages. Instead, they are ideas for magazine articles of 2,000 words. To determine if you have enough to say for a book, try taking your topic and dividing it into ten to fifteen chapters. Would you be able to write fifteen to twenty manuscript pages worth of information for each of those chapters? Does each chapter have its own special theme? Do you have lists of how-to tips, charts, quizzes, and worksheets that provide vital information and occupy manuscript space?

If you have enough material to warrant a book-length work, be tough on your idea and ask yourself if it is marketable. Try writing a two-paragraph description of the book that a publisher might use for back-of-the-book sales copy. Is your book salable? Does it attract a specific, clearly defined audience? What's new about what you have to say?

Once you are certain that you've got a strong book idea, write a two-page query letter to a literary agent. The letter should begin with an interest-grabbing lead, like any query letter, and then describe the book, its potential readers, and the void your book fills when compared to what's currently available. Names of agents and the types of books they represent can be found in the library in one of several reference books. *Literary Agents of North America* and *Literary Marketplace* are two good sources; your librarian may know of others. Read the descriptions of the agents and find one or more who represents the type of work you want to write. You'll most likely be writing nonfiction, so don't send your idea to a fiction-only agent and don't send a business book idea to someone who specializes in science and medicine.

Unlike the magazine proposal, it is appropriate to send your book query letter to more than one agent at a time. If several are interested in representing your book idea, choose the agent who you feel is most in tune with your book topic, who has the best track record in selling books for top dollar, and whose personality clicks with yours.

Your agent will ask for yet another proposal to send to editors at publishing houses. This proposal runs from ten to fifty pages and includes the following:

- Book Overview—summarizes your idea and how the book will be written. Will it include real-life anecdotes, quotes from experts in the field, worksheets, graphs, or illustrations?

- Marketing Statement—describes the audience for the book and the timeliness of the idea and lists four to six other books that yours will compete with. Don't say that no other book has been written on the subject quite like yours. Instead find the books that are closest to yours and write a paragraph about those books and how yours differs or how it clarifies or improves what has previously been written on the subject.

- Table of Contents

- Chapter Summaries—outlines, in one or two paragraphs, what you will say in each chapter.

- Two Sample Chapters—Gives a sample of your information and writing style. It's best to pick two chapters other than the first and the second. Choose the most significant and important chapters to write as samples to let your expertise shine through.

- Author Bio—describes your background as it pertains to the subject and lists any previous writing credits.

Once your agent has had you make any changes in the proposal, he or she will send it off with a cover letter to a number of potential publishing houses. Responses from publishers can take anywhere from a few weeks if your topic sizzles to several months if it requires more convincing.

A publisher will offer an advance for the book that can range anywhere from a few thousand dollars to many thousand dollars and a percentage of royalties, that ranges from about 8 to 12 percent. Publishing is not the road to getting rich quick. In fact, to understand the harsh realities of the field, read *The Awful Truth About Publishing* by John Boswell (Warner Books, New York, 1986). But even if your book is a loss leader, the potential it holds to establish you as an authority and to help you win speaking engagements and new business is remarkable. And there are few business joys that match being asked to sign a book that bears your byline as the expert in the field.

Self-Publishing Puts You in Charge

If you don't have the time to interest a publisher in your book or to wait for the publishing house to edit, design, and print it, you may want to consider self-publishing. Getting your work typeset—or having it converted from your word-processing disk into desktop publishing form—and printed can often be quicker when you take control. You don't have to worry about an editor reworking your material or a designer you've never met creating a cover design that reminds you more of a Most-Wanted poster than a book jacket. And since you should be hiring professional freelance help—editors, designers, and printers—you don't lose in getting input from the publishing field.

While publishing houses pay you for your book, in self-publishing you foot the bill for editing, typesetting, printing, and marketing. Don't, however, get self-publishing confused with vanity presses, which have earned questionable reputations for charging anxious authors large sums of money to print their books.

Marian K. Woodall, a speech coach, realized that she needed a book that capsulized twenty-five years of material she had developed while teaching business communications on the college level. She came up with the title, *Thinking on Your Feet*, and created a separate publishing company to produce the book.

Woodall has five primary reasons for publishing her own books, what she calls independent publishing.

1. Maintain control of decisions on the title, color, and quality of the printing.

2. Expedite publishing.

3. Earn more money.

4. Keep the book in print longer.

5. Sell the books at seminars and give them to her clients without having to buy the book back from the publisher.

"I give my books away every chance I can as a promotional tool for my company," says Woodall. "When I make a sales call as a speech coach for executives, there is nothing better I can leave behind than a copy of *Speaking to a Group*. I couldn't afford to do that if I had to buy the book from the publisher."

Woodall can get a book out in the time it takes a publisher to make a decision whether or not to buy your idea. She produced her book, *How to Talk So Men Will Listen*, in just over five months.

"The publishing itself is a manufacturing process," she contends. "There is nothing magical about having a third party say your material is worth publishing. For too long, writers have felt that their work isn't validated unless a major house publishes it. I'd like to destigmatize independent publishing and encourage more people to take advantage of it to get their message out quickly and conveniently."

To reduce time marketing her books, Woodall interests national organizations, such as Toastmasters International, and small presses that publish books in her field of expertise to include her book in their publishing lists. "*Thinking on Your Feet* sold to ten catalogs around the country, two library distributors, and a Canadian one, plus I have just begun to interest chain bookstores in buying it," she says.

Earning Newspaper Bylines

The standard way to get your company's name in the newspaper is to send a news release, which smaller papers may print verbatim and which larger ones may use as fodder for an article that quotes you and several other sources. For local publicity, there are alternatives.

The opinion-editorial page of your newspaper is filled each day with guest editorials from persons within your community who have something significant to say on a particular topic. Become familiar with that page. By following the editorials, you may find that something has been written that stirs your ire or makes you want to add to or clarify a previously published piece. That's your cue to write to the editor to share your insight in a field or your passion about a topic.

Don't view the opinion-editorial page as just a place to air grievances. Its purpose is to express thoughtful opinions on a wide range of topics. While unloading biases may be cathartic while you're alone at your computer, tomorrow your potential customers are going to judge your business by what you say. If you have a particularly strong view on a subject, write the piece and then let it cool for a day. Then ask an unbiased colleague for his or her opinion. You want your writing and your message to be strong. Although hate mail may sell more newspapers, it can turn off the business that it is meant to attract.

The president of a major league baseball team was concerned about a local opinion survey. Area residents believed that the team was not run in a business-like manner and that it cared little for the community. One of the most intriguing comments to come out of the study came from a business leader who said that the team was like a public utility—it was the only baseball team in town. In other words, the team didn't care because it didn't have to care.

Many steps had been taken in the previous years to improve the business operations of the team, but they had never been communicated to the public. Using a professional writer, the president produced an opinion piece, which was published in the local newspaper.

The piece began with a quote from Yogi Berra: "If the people don't want to come out to the park, nobody's going to stop them." He cited the public utility comment, but explained he did not have a monopoly on the entertainment dollar. The team competed not with the rest of the league, but with other sporting events, movies, plays, concerts, and museums.

After explaining the steps the team was taking to improve its business operations, the president concluded by stating his mission: to generate a product that a public utility would be proud of—a team so good that 99 percent of the people want and need it. Copies of the opinion piece were then circulated with a note to important audiences of the team, including government leaders who controlled the stadium, season ticket holders, employees, vendors, and members of the media.

In addition to occasionally responding to a piece on the opinion-editorial page, consider writing on an original topic. The nice part about opinion pieces is that they are just that—opinions. You don't have to spend weeks doing research or finding anecdotes to fill the pages of a magazine. But you do need to have something worthwhile to say that will show your integrity, dedication, and passion about your point of view. Statistics that can pin down points will add muscle to your message.

To draw attention to his professional society's work to help the homeless, for example, the president of a psychiatric society drafted a letter to the editor on the plight of the homeless in his city. He cited numbers of homeless, percentages of those who suffered from mental illness, and dollars being spent by the city to care for them. He outlined what members of the society were doing to help and how the entire city could respond to impact the problem. The letter helped to position the society on a topic important to its constituents. And rather than assuming that those who needed to know the society's position read the paper that morning, the president sent copies of the editorial with brief, personally written cover notes to key players in the psychiatric field.

Daily newspapers traditionally only include nonstaff or nonjournalist bylines in the opinion-editorial section, but some community newspapers, business publications, and daily advertising supplements print bylined articles from professionals. Submit your ideas to these editors in a personalized query letter.

If you're unsure what supplements a daily or business newspaper has planned, call an editorial assistant to find out. The newspaper may have a yearly calendar listing its supplements. Be certain that you learn who the editor is for the supplement, because it is often not the same person who edits the regular publication, and the person may rotate on a quarterly or yearly basis.

Sharon Lacy, the president of a family business consulting firm, wrote the article, "Shaking Loose Some Startup Cash from Your (Family) Money Tree," for a supplement of the *San Diego Business Journal*. She paid Diane several hundred dollars to edit an 800-word article. That investment earned three new clients and several supportive letters to the editor about her piece that now supplements her new business packet of promotional materials.

For a health care supplement to the *San Diego Business Journal*, Diane also ghostwrote two articles for her clients, owners of an employee-assistance program in San Diego. Diane pitched one article idea on helping employees cope with catastrophic illness in the workplace to the editor. While on the phone selling that idea, the editor liked what she heard about the company and assigned a second article on how to choose a doctor. The articles positioned the company as a leader in the field and included a brief bio on each author. The $900 cost for ghostwriting two articles generated two bylined pieces that the client has used to mail to prospective clients as well as to serve as clippings to show trade journal editors that they have a publishing track record.

Blanketing the Market with White Papers

Writing a white paper or an overview on a subject allows you to self-publish an article or report that can be mailed to key prospects or referrals in your field to establish your credibility and authority on a topic. They can also preempt yet-to-be published articles in newspapers, magazines, or trade journals to record that you were first to evaluate a problem in a certain way or to identify key solutions. Remember, however, that your white paper should not be simply a copy of a manuscript you have sent to a publication. Having potential readers see your article prior to publication does neither you nor the magazine any favors. But it can be a report on the same topic with some of the same statistics.

In some cases, you may simply send the paper as an "FYI" to your target audience. This is a way of keeping in touch and offering valuable information on a topic. In other instances, white papers are offered as incentives to your public to take action, whether it be to fill out a survey or to mail back a reply card in a direct mail order.

A human resource consultant offered a white paper on gainsharing to company CEOs and human resource directors, who took the time to fill out and mail back a questionnaire surveying what companies were looking for in contract human resource services. The offer, coupled with the chance to win a signed and numbered lithograph, yielded a better than 10 percent response rate.

As part of a direct mail campaign to bolster its speakers' bureau, one employee assistance company offered two white papers—one on drug abuse in the workplace and the other on avoiding burnout—to anyone who mailed back a business reply card requesting more detail on its speakers.

Merchandizing Your Writing

The primary way to get the most mileage from a published article is to send it with cover letters to potential prospects or to use it in new business presentation packets. Articles can also be mailed to current clients to offer useful information on a topic of interest and to establish your credibility.

Bylined articles or chapters from a book you've written can also be used as handouts for speeches or for college or extension courses that you teach. Once the seminar attendee gets back to his or her office and reviews materials or shares it with the boss, wouldn't you prefer that key decision makers refer to your article on the topic rather than one by some unknown author who may be your competitor?

Best of all, the more you write on a topic, the more you increase your chances of writing for more and more prestigious publications. Bylines beget bylines. Editors of major magazines and publishing houses are more likely to take a chance on having you write for them if you have tested your talents first in local newspapers or trade journals.

Call attention to your publishing credentials in your bio in your company's flyers and brochures. An attorney, who was one of the first in the country to conduct living trust seminars, marketed a new breed of seminars by touting the fact that articles quoting him had appeared in such prestigious publications as *Money*, the *Wall Street Journal*, *US News & World Report* and *Newsweek*.

There's No Trick to Finding Ghost Writers

If writing for you is, as a late *New York Times* sportswriter put it, "easy... you just sit down at a typewriter and open a vein," then the tourniquet for you may be a ghost writer or collaborator.

There is a plethora of professional writers who are eager to find good ghost-writing assignments. Finding them just takes understanding of how such writers get their work. A good place to start is with a professional writers' association in your community. The library, bookstores, university English or journalism departments, or your local paper may know of the writers' organizations in your town. If not, chances are a local public relations, marketing, or advertising agency may know.

A number of professional societies include job information hot lines or job referral services that can match you with a writer who has special expertise or understanding in your field. Independent Writers of Southern California, for example, has chapters in Los Angeles and San Diego, both of which can give interested parties the names and telephone numbers of scores of good writers. Other independent writers' organizations exist throughout the country. Public relations or other communications professionals organizations, such as PRSA (Public Relations Society of America) or IABC (International Association of Business Communicators) also often offer job lines that can carry your need for a ghost writer.

Nationally, the American Society of Journalists and Authors based in New York City features Dial-a-Writer, a service that provides you with the names and telephone numbers of writers qualified to handle your project. You pay nothing for the service; the writer pays a percentage of the fee he or she earns.

Literary agents are another good source for writers. Some agencies may give you the name of several writers who can help you polish your prose into a marketable work that the agent would then try to sell. Journalism departments at colleges and universities may employ professors who write for consumer magazines and books, or a professor may refer you to a prize student.

The difference between a ghost writer and collaborator is how visible the writer is on the book jacket. Typically, a ghost writer is one whose name doesn't appear on the front of the book but is included in an acknowledgment in the first few pages of the book. A collaborator is one who is recognized under the title as a coauthor either with a byline that reads "By (Your Name) and (Collaborator's Name)" or "By (Your Name) with (Collaborator's Name)."

No matter the prominence of the byline, writers don't come cheap. You may be lucky to find a good, hungry writer who is trying to break into magazines or book publishing who is willing to work on the come. That person may settle for a percentage of the fee once the work is sold. But, typically, you'll get to work that way only once with that author.

Any writer who earns his or her living writing soon discovers that while he or she is writing for nothing, you, the expert, are earning a living in your field. You have an income and a book. The writer has only a byline. Recognizing that writing is a profession only if he or she can earn a living, a good writer will charge an hourly or project fee to ghostwrite or collaborate. Fees vary, but an average hourly ranges between $35 and $75. Magazine articles may be written for as little as a few hundred to as much as several thousand dollars. And book proposals' flat fees can reach as high as $3,000 to $5,000.

Newsweek writer Charles Leerhsen, who wrote Donald Trump's second autobiography, received a fee that publishing sources say was in the mid six figures. *Trump: Surviving at the Top* was a collaboration with a byline that read by Donald Trump with Charles Leerhsen.

While Leerhsen received no royalties with his big fee, most writers not earning top dollar will want a percentage of the advance or royalties. While you won't want to offer more than you can afford, letting the writer have a stake in the book's outcome generally guarantees that more effort will go into producing a top-quality work.

Getting published is an important variable in the self-marketing success quotient. Don't let the excuse that you're not a good writer prevent you from earning a byline. What is essential and can never be farmed out, however, is your ability to present quality information and ideas. Your material should spark an "ah ha" in your readers and ignite them to reach greater heights. If you can prompt someone else to succeed, then you will have too.

Top Self-Marketing Secrets

How to Get Published

1. Sell angles, not ideas, that shout "new and intriguing."

2. Create a sizzling title that's so hot readers can't pass it up. Use puns, cliches, and even the rhyme of songs to get you thinking.

3. Summarize your article idea in a query letter to sell an editor *before* you write the article.

4. Target your message to a specific audience by selling articles to trade journals.

5. Write a book—it's the ultimate credibility builder.

6. Start your book by writing a two-page query letter to an agent.

7. Sell a publisher on your idea with a book proposal that spells out the book's unique angle and sales potential.

8. Consider independent publishing to get your book out fast and to maintain control.

9. Write a newspaper opinion piece to express thoughtful opinions you want customers and supporters to read.

10. Send informational white papers to clients and prospects to demonstrate expertise and authority in your field.

11. Merchandise your writing: Send copies of articles and books to decision makers to build credibility and to give them valuable information. If you prompt someone else to succeed, you will have too.

12. If you don't like to write or don't have time, hire a ghost writer to turn your thoughts into prose.

8

Speak Up and Often
A Platform for Increased Prospecting

Feeling nervous before stepping up to give a speech in front of a roomful of unfamiliar faces is natural. As Lily Tomlin said, "We're all in this alone." The fact that your knees buckle and your vocal chords tighten when you think about public speaking is no excuse for not using this powerful vehicle to propel yourself into a new sphere of influence. Public speaking is unequivocally the foremost fear among Americans; it is also one of the most powerful ways to market yourself and your business.

Before giving into your fear, ask yourself what you are afraid of. A University of Michigan study showed that 60 percent of our fears are totally unwarranted, 20 percent have already become past activities, and 10 percent are so petty that they make no difference. Of the remaining 10 percent, only 5 percent are real and justifiable. In other words, there is a twenty-to-one chance that any fear you have of tripping up at the podium is not based on fact, but on having the wrong focus. It's not what happens *to* you that matters but what happens *inside* you that counts. What you believe determines what you receive.

The most important element of successful public speaking is knowledge about your subject. That, coupled with pointers from pros and sheer determination to overcome stage fright or the imposter syndrome, will allow you to become a sought-after speaker. Instead of buying advertisements to tout your expertise, you'll be paid to share it with others and you'll win new leads.

Positioning yourself as an expert in a field by giving talks on a subject is the ultimate soft sell. Rather than your asking for an appointment with someone, your prospects have made the decision to invest time and money to come hear *you*.

Ronald Kent, president of a mutual fund and partner in a small brokerage firm in Kailua, Hawaii, is an engineer turned stockbroker. Although he was successful as a senior engineer for Aerojet General, he realized he was making more money fiddling with stocks on his lunch hour than working all day at his drafting table. So Kent switched careers and started selling high-quality blue chip stocks. But, as a reserved engineer who shrivels when someone turns him down for lunch, Kent knew he needed to promote himself in a way that provided a path of least resistance. Speaking became the one way he could sell without making cold calls on strangers.

"I knew I'd never overcome my fear of rejection, so I invested my creative energy into finding ways to sell where I couldn't be rejected," says Kent. "I began speaking about investing as a way to let people know who I was, what I was about, and what I believed. Those who liked what I said and wanted me as their stockbroker would seek me out after my talk. I didn't have to worry about those who weren't interested." When you're the speaker, people seek *you* out. What a refreshing change in the sales cycle.

Make the College Classroom Your Test Lab

Securing speaking engagements is not as easy as throwing your name into the hat. You have to prove that you have a business track record, a unique message worth hearing, and compelling speaking skills. Before taking your show on the road, think about starting in a safer environment—the college extended studies program. You need valuable credentials for a college or university to consider you for a position; but you have the advantage of preparing for a multiweek course, perhaps using a textbook, and speaking in an environment in which lecture notes are acceptable.

Both authors of this book have used this platform to establish their credibility and expertise and to earn business. For Diane, the step up to the podium didn't come easily. An eighth grade drama teacher's comment that her voice quivered and she'd never make it on the stage stayed with Diane until age thirty. Even holding corporate public relations positions, being interviewed by television reporters, and addressing boards of directors didn't put her at ease in front of an audience.

Finally, in 1984, when Diane sold her book, *Get Published: Top Editors Tell You How,* she realized that to increase book sales, she had to go on the circuit and talk about it. The first time Diane addressed a roomful of people in Austin, Texas, she prepared a power-packed speech filled with pithy quotes from top national magazine editors and useful how-tos for would-be writers. But instead of telling the audience what she had learned from the most prominent editors in the country, she read her speech. Every single word. When one attendee wrote in his evaluation, "Diane, just talk to us," the author-turned-speaker realized that she'd better practice speaking in public if she wanted to sell herself and her books.

Diane started simply. She signed up with a private education and seminar company and offered a course on selling to the top national magazines in the comfort of her living room. With an audience of a dozen or so friendly faces to whom she served tea and cookies, Diane felt safe and free to talk easily about what she knew.

With that first successful step, she gave talks on publishing to professional public relations, marketing, and writing organizations. Back-of-the-room sales of *Get Published* made the endeavor worth the time. Positive comments from the audience about her understanding of the field spurred her on.

After a talk to the Public Relations Club of San Diego, a member of the audience who worked at the University of California, San Diego (UCSD), passed along Diane's name to the director of the writing program for the Extended Studies College. That referral resulted in her teaching for five years at UCSD and serving as director of two major writers' conferences hosted by the University.

In addition to being paid to talk about her first love, Diane overcame her speaking jitters and learned how to work an audience using humor, personal stories—including professional foibles, which audiences love—and practical information that can turn around careers. She gained recognition as an authority on national magazine publishing and book writing. Students she met in class often became clients for her public relations and marketing company, and others who repeatedly noted her name in the catalog called upon her as an expert writing consultant.

Diane has spoken on publishing at writers' conferences nationwide and on public relations and marketing to corporations, associations, women's rallies, and the chamber of commerce. But one goal remains: to track down that junior high drama teacher and let her know that even an audience of 500 can't make Diane's voice quiver today.

Henry took a similar tack to establish his expertise and to earn new business. He taught through the Learning Annex and UCSD Extension to position himself as a marketing guru. The catalog listing his class and instructor biography reached 100,000 people each quarter and proved better exposure than the Yellow Pages. Many businesspeople use the catalog to find speakers on specific subjects. One resultant speaking engagement for Henry generated a $1 million account for the public relations and advertising agency where he was vice president.

Additional speaking stints, such as one-night-a-week classes or Saturday morning seminars on "How to Make Your Business Famous" and "How to Get Big Results on a Small Advertising Budget," generated additional invitations for his agency to bid on accounts they probably wouldn't have heard about otherwise. And every presentation he has done for the chamber of commerce on marketing businesses has generated at least one new business lead. Henry believes that the more times you present your company to prospective clients, the closer you get to landing the next big account.

Charles Mann, a personal financial adviser, also taps the extended studies market to attract corporate clients. He regularly gives financial seminars through university extended studies programs. The sessions are strictly informative, and there is no hard sell of him or his firm. However, all the handouts are photocopied on his stationery that includes his phone number. Mann receives most of his clients from these efforts. It appears that extension students seem to be more motivated, better educated, and more attuned to forming alliances than the average person in the industry.

Tie into Your Chamber and Move Out from There

Providing opportunities for businesses to succeed is part and parcel of the chamber of commerce, and therefore an excellent place to become known as a speaker. Chambers of commerce typically host workshops and seminars for members and are always looking for presenters who will offer inspiring, insightful how-to's in exchange for exposure and heightened credibility.

Take time to get to know the individuals who coordinate seminars for the chamber. But realize that few things come without a price tag. You will need to volunteer for committees and task forces to demonstrate your commitment and expertise. Then, when you've made inroads, let your desire be known to speak to professional groups.

Jeanine Just, owner of Kreative Solutions in Laguna Beach, California, used the local chamber to book speaking engagements after leaving the corporate world to found her own "success" coaching company. "I wanted to position myself with the path of least resistance, so I went to the president of the chamber of commerce and told him what I did," says Just. "He slipped me in as an expert for an upcoming program."

Making the leap from an arena where you are known, such as your own professional organization or the chamber, to the corporate world and other professional associations, takes marketing know-how. In addition to using contacts to get your foot in the door, a creatively designed and expertly written speaker's bureau brochure and personalized cover letter can serve as an entrée. Include a business reply card on which potential clients can check off the topic they are interested in and request that you call to set up an appointment. Once your brochure has been in the hands of prospects for a week or two, follow up with a phone call. Work to secure an appointment to present yourself and your topic and to demonstrate the new approach or information you have to share.

With her awareness established through the chamber, Just began contacting corporations directly to provide private success coaching and training programs. She calls her approach educational marketing. Rather than give a hard sell, Just educates companies about her unique niche in the marketplace and how her service strengthens employees' skills. "I have a service that is new and needs explanation," says Just. "They need to experience me to understand my philosophy and approach." Over the six years she has been in business for herself, Just has made strong connections throughout the country and is now beginning to become internationally known. As she grew professionally, she asked for larger and larger speaking engagements. Three years ago, she landed a talk for Senator William Campbell's conference and was billed with Oprah Winfrey and Mrs. Anwar el-Sadat. More than 14,000 participants packed the conference and heard Just's speech, "Self-Worth: Your Ultimate Power." The result? Within three months, Just was performing warm-up acts and break-out sessions for Elizabeth Dole's political conferences during the 1988 presidential campaign, when her husband, Bob Dole, was vying for the Republican nomination.

"Initially I spoke for just an honorarium, but within a few years I worked up to almost $1,000 plus expenses per speech, and it won't be long before I'm commanding $2,500 per presentation. Just started out as a consultant who used speaking as a marketing technique to attract new clients. Today, 50 percent of her business is private coaching and 50 percent is public seminars. She expects that, within another few years, she will earn most of her income as a professional speaker. With a goal of $25,000 per hour-long talk (not unheard of for the cream of the crop), she'll no doubt be living well.

That brings up a point. As someone marketing your business through speaking engagements, should you charge a fee to speak? Yes, but not when you are launching your career and not always even after you've become established.

"I did free speeches when I first started speaking to promote my business, and I still do because we all owe something back for the opportunities we've been given," says Marian K. Woodall, who created Professional Business Communications after a twenty-five-year career teaching college. "But it's important for anyone who says they are enough of an expert to give a speech and who has the qualifications, to ask for an honorarium when appropriate. You wouldn't ask a doctor to come perform a little surgery over lunch, in exchange for a plate of chicken and rice. Those professionals who tend to speak for free make it hard for professional speakers to get the fees appropriate for their expertise."

There are times when you want to give away your talent. Save pro bono work for your own professional organization, for the chamber of commerce who has referred business to you, and for charity. Otherwise, once you've established yourself as an expert, charge a fee, however small.

A television reporter for the Fox network has a policy that she will not serve as a keynote speaker or master of ceremonies without an honorarium. She doesn't have a set fee schedule; she leaves the payment to the discretion of the sponsoring company or organization. That honorarium policy has enhanced her stature and trimmed her bookings to groups that really want and appreciate her.

Offer Free, Informative Seminars to Attract Clients

You don't have to wait for an invitation to speak to have a platform for your wares. Hosting a self-sponsored seminar or workshop is equally valuable to your prospects and your business. There's a plethora of financial planners holding investment seminars and attorneys sponsoring living trust seminars. Real estate brokers offer free workshops on how to buy a condo or how to get the most value from home fixer-upper projects. These workshops are typically offered at no charge or for a nuisance fee of five or ten dollars to weed out the Lookie Lou's from those serious about the subject—and ideally those who would be better prospects of coming back to the speaker for consulting services.

Jean Nave, owner of Motivational Dynamics and author of three books, including *Women: The World's Greatest Salesmen*, left her position as marketing director for a computer firm to launch her own sales training company. She set her sights on having corporations book her for in-house training. To get her feet wet and to earn leads, she offered off-site seminars on how to decide if a career in sales is for you. She booked a room at a local hotel for $100 for a half day and charged $35 a person for the seminar. She spent $20 on printing flyers, which she distributed to corporations, primarily through the administrative secretaries. "In most cases, since my original topic was centered around my book and women in sales, I was able to interest the secretary in the program herself, and once she bought into it, it was easy to get the flyers posted," says Nave.

Nave marketed her seminars to women who seemed frustrated by their careers, including nurses and teachers. "I knew from the research I did for my book that women in nursing were well educated but frustrated with their careers, and teachers were also intelligent individuals but underpaid for their ability," explains Nave. "My seminars let them evaluate if sales was for them and gave them tips on how to sell. I filled the seminar each time, and most of the women who attended were from large corporations, so they later became my connections to book corporate seminars."

After hosting ten seminars of her own, for which she made about $1,000 or better a day, Nave had the entrée she needed to take her talks in-house. Today, eight years later, she is still getting calls from individuals who attended one of her original seminars. "They liked what I did and hung on to my name," says Nave.

Nave says that what makes her memorable is that she that she is completely original. "I didn't read what anyone else was doing in sales training when I started," she says. "Instead I looked inside at what I had been doing as a coach, manager, and self-motivator. Then I poured out what I did and developed a seminar around it."

After starting with the obvious night school and university classes and moving on to speaking to corporations, stockbroker Ronald Kent decided to find new ways to spread his reputation. He did the unthinkable and approached his competitors. Like Dracula taking care of the blood bank, he convinced savings and loans, banks, and federal credit unions that his conservative philosophy was consistent with theirs. Time and again, these financial institutions have sponsored Kent to present programs for their depositors. "The fact that I sold them on the idea is one thing; but that they have asked me back over and over makes me even more proud," says Kent.

To find other nontraditional routes to market his services, Kent also convinced a leading department store in Honolulu that had just opened a fine restaurant to invite its best customers to an exclusive dinner meeting about personal finance. The dinners were so well received, that they grew into luncheon programs.

When strictly women showed up for the luncheons, Kent turned that into a sales tactic and began advertising them as women-only investment programs. The year was 1965, and since Kent was the first to offer women such an opportunity—the media attention alone was worth his time and energy.

Today, Kent gives fifty to sixty speeches a year. But he controls whom he attracts by creating talk titles that will bias an audience. "I want to appeal to the type of individuals who would make good clients for me," says Kent. "I don't want traders, speculators, or get-rich quickers. My titles appeal to the conservative and stodgy. Hot shots don't sign up for seminars entitled, 'Gentlemen Prefer Bonds,' 'The Feeling Is Mutual,' or 'Realistic Investments for the Cautious Investor.'"

Kent doesn't view speaking as a shortcut to making the sale. In fact, he often doesn't reap immediate rewards. "It's not uncommon for new clients to tell me that they heard me speak ten years ago, and that a recent inheritance or home sale prompted them to remember that they liked what I had said and decided to come in to talk."

Today, as a member of the National Speakers' Association, Kent sells his speaking talent as much as his financial expertise. His most popular topic for the noninvestor audience is developing creativity for problem solving. If people want to speak to promote themselves or their business, Kent advises them to tap into their creative reservoir to develop a personal trademark. When you're first starting as a speaker, learn the traditional, recognized approaches to the business, he says. Then figure out what makes you unique and go with your strengths.

What makes Kent a sought-after speaker is his ability to excite the audience. "I can talk about the mildest subject, but people come out thinking they've just had a revelation," says Kent. "After analyzing tapes of myself, I realized that my speaking style triggers something in the minds of people listening to me that sets them on their own internal journey. It's much like the talent of an inspiring church minister. It's the exciting stuff going on inside their own heads that makes them think I'm a terrific speaker. In reality, I'm just the catalyst."

Channel Nervous Energy

Zig Ziglar, an all-star in the big league of motivational speakers, says that if you put a mule on stage, it will stand there unimpressed, not thinking a thing about the crowd and bright lights. But if you put a thoroughbred horse in the same situation, it will pace nervously, balk, and whinny.

It's natural to be high-strung and self-conscious when you put yourself in front of an audience that expects you to entertain, inform, out-knowledge, and out-experience them in the field. If you're a champion like the thoroughbred, expect to be jittery, but learn to channel that nervousness into positive energy.

Just like an airplane pilot views flight time, remember that the more you speak in public, the better you'll get. Teaching college courses, for which you have to prepare lesson plans and present week after week for six weeks or three months, is a perfect arena in which to practice. One of the benefits of teaching is that teachers always learn more than students. Knowing you have to face thirty students once or twice a week forces you to research your material and have enough to say to fill the time slot. Night by night you'll become more and more comfortable speaking to a group, and you'll know your material so well that having to rely on notes will become a thing of the past.

To quickly win over a classroom of students, Henry makes it his trademark to learn every single student's name the first night of class. Since all memorization is repetition and association, he repeats the student's name a number of times in a row in conversation and then tries to exaggerate the name in his mind by associating it with something funny or memorable. When he came across a student in his class named Noonie, he thought of the movie *High Noon* with Gary Cooper. (By the way, Noonie was so memorable that Henry and Diane asked her to serve as editor of this book.) Henry set the record one night when he perfectly memorized sixty-eight students' names in twenty minutes.

If you can't teach a class before you launch your speaking career, you can at least offer your services as a guest lecturer to undergraduate college classes. Local professors in your field are excellent persons to form linkages with, and you'll be doing them a favor by volunteering to lecture to one of their classes.

A professor frequently asks Diane to be a guest lecturer for his magazine article writing class. After several speeches, the professor recommended Diane to the editor of a local trade journal, who subsequently assigned thousands of dollars worth of writing to her company. In turn, the professor has served as a guest speaker at the writing classes Diane teaches.

If you don't have the opportunity to use college classes as a way to build your speaking skills, at least practice your craft in front of colleagues at work or family and friends. Prior to giving a new talk, Henry assembles a half dozen unassuming office mates and lures them to listen to his speech by buying them a soda.

Practicing in front of a live audience is essential. Rehearsing telling jokes and anecdotes in front of a friendly crowd will help you to get the rhythm and pace of the story. If there is a punch line, play with the emphasis to see which variation gets the biggest reaction. The same holds true for a serious or especially moving story.

To make sure she knows her material well, Jean Nave reads her material into a tape recorder and then plays the tape continually to herself for two weeks prior to her speaking date. "By the time I go on stage, it's as though I have given this speech thirty to forty times before," she explains. "I have internalized the information so that it flows easily from me. I abhor memorized speeches because they are not natural, but knowing your material well so that you can easily recall statistics and anecdotes makes you look like a pro."

Research the Audience to Identify Desires

There are few things as nerve-racking as looking at the blank stares of an audience and wondering if what you're saying addresses their interests and experience. Rather than guessing whether your speech meets the audience's needs, talk to a few members of the organization before you prepare your speech.

Ask the individual who booked you to suggest key members of the group or business that you can contact. Call these people and find out about the group and what it wants from your talk. Contacted individuals will feel honored that you've taken the time to ask for their opinion. And they'll give you good pointers for the direction of your speech.

If polling a number of members won't fit into your schedule, ask the program chairperson to fill out a questionnaire you've designed to identify points of interest and concern the group would like you to address. Quest Management Consultants of Bonsall, California, sends out a pre-program questionnaire that includes information such as

> number of attendees—males/females
> average age
> job responsibilities
> session objectives
> key issues to discuss/to avoid
> name and title of introducer
> start and end time for your talk

And while we're talking about sending things ahead to the program chairperson, always remember to get the request for your talk in writing—whether or not you are being paid to speak. To make things easy, prepare an agreement in which the person who "hires" you simply has to fill in the blanks (time, date, location, program title, and speaker's fee), sign and date it, and return it to you.

Another way to feel more at ease with the group you'll be speaking to is to arrive early at the seminar or speech site. Jean Nave makes it a point to always arrive at her talks a half hour early so that she can mix with the people and incorporate discussion into her speech. That kind of intimate knowledge shows that she is one of the fold, in tune with the audience's needs.

Jeanine Just of Kreative Solutions says she honors the attendees who come to her talks by asking them why they came and what they want to learn. "I'm not a canned speaker; I never say the same thing twice," says Just. "Instead of inflicting information on the audience, I identify their needs and then, through an interactive, participative session, we all laugh and commiserate together, and we all come away knowing more than when we started."

Armed with inside knowledge, you can feel more at ease from the moment you step into the room where your speech will take place. First, you are no longer a stranger; you've already established a phone relationship with a handful of individuals in the audience. Find out who those individuals are and take the time, before you go on, to introduce yourself. Being able to spot a few familiar faces in a sea of unknowns will help relax you as you speak. And when you address the audience, you can let them know that you have talked to members of the group with comments like, "George Bryce said the most essential piece of information he wanted to learn today was...." or "Candace Higgins said that a major concern many of you have is...."

Your audience will be impressed that you cared enough about their needs to do your homework. And because you did, your speech will be easier to make and more valued. Encore! Encore!

Getting Started: Make Your Warm-up Sizzle

Grab the interest of your audience with a great introduction. There are a number of approaches that work as lead statements. Choose the one that works best for your particular subject and speaking style. Here is how a member of the Building Industry Association would address a roomful of developers using each of the speech lead options.

- Direct Statement
  San Diego is at a crossroads. The San Diego we love will vanish if we don't find solutions.

- Engaging Question
  If you could wave a magic wand and solve one problem in San Diego, which problem would you choose? Let's talk about solutions that are right for San Diego, the environment, the economy, and future generations.

- Pertinent Quote
  Henry Ford once said: 'Don't find fault. Find a remedy.' Today, let's explore some remedies for San Diego.

- Shocking Statement
  If we don't do something now, America's Finest City will become America's Finest Mess.

- Humorous Incident
  Whatever works for you. Humor is personal.

- Human Interest Story
  Travel back in time to a century ago. The year is 1891. A thirty-six-year-old Illinois native arrives by steam locomotive at the Santa Fe Depot in San Diego. He heads north by horse and buggy and comes across a barren high mesa of land. Acting as his own architect, he constructs roads, plants trees, creates ponds, and begins building a home. It was to have forty-seven rooms and all of the grandeur of a California hacienda. He called it Miramar, after a castle outside of Trieste. Today we call this area Scripps Ranch. Building homes was a lot easier when newspaper tycoon E. W. Scripps arrived in San Diego.

Let Them Eat Candy: Your Style Precedes You

You've got to have something valuable to say to earn an audience's attention, but to keep it takes style and pizazz. To keep head-nodding and eye-glazing to a minimum, you must command attention.

Henry exudes energy every time he speaks. The first thing he does when he rushes up to the podium after an introduction is to turn on a kitchen timer and set it on top of the lectern. That simple gesture lets audience members know that Henry respects their time. It also shows that he knows he's working under a deadline and that when the timer sounds, he'll stop. The audience senses from the beginning that Henry must have a lot to say and that there's no way he'd waste time on unimportant information.

Next, Henry passes out handouts that highlight the main points of his presentation, with blanks for important points and statistics that the audience will fill in. This keeps people on their toes, yet not tied to taking rote notes. They know that they can just listen, but if they want the most from the information, they'll be filling in the blanks and keeping pace with Henry.

Henry never returns to the podium. He moves out into the audience, even if it is several hundred people large. And just in case anyone isn't paying attention, Henry throws out a question. When someone volunteers an answer or an anecdote, he quickly reaches into a bag of tricks, and tosses out a candy bar stadium-vendor style to the lucky respondent—filling the house with laughter and keeping the audience on its toes. To keep in step with the healthy lifestyle, he now also throws apples and oranges.

The treat-tossing antics consistently score high marks on Henry's presentation evaluations. Since studies show that people retain 90 percent of what they say compared to 10 percent of what they hear, the reward–participation technique makes Henry's speeches interactive and people remember him for it. And, since it's what his audiences like best, he keeps giving them what they want.

Handouts are also an important part of talks presented by Jeanine Just. "People want information they can take back with them, and handouts are perfect for that," she says. "I always make sure that the handouts include humor because if the presentation isn't fun, you can forget it as a speaker." And most likely, the audience won't remember you.

Jean Nave, owner of Motivational Dynamics, makes sure her handouts are keepers by including quotes penned in calligraphy. "I'm a collector of quotes, and so are many other people," says Nave. "Attractively written quotes get posted, and when that happens, so does my name on the top of the handout. It's advertising that brings me business."

Other presentation aids are also important to keep your audience involved. It's been said that 87 percent of what people learn comes from sight, and that the remaining 13 percent of learning is divided into hearing (7 percent), smell (3.5 percent), touch (1.5 percent), and taste (1 percent). Flip charts using brightly colored markers, overhead transparencies (try yellow and blue instead of white), chalkboards, and short videotapes are other visual media that can help you drive home your points. Just remember to keep visual aids simple—one idea per slide or overhead is plenty. You can also make use of role playing, small group discussion demonstrations, short true or false quizzes, and even children's stories, puzzles, and games to help your audience discover for themselves what you are trying to impart.

Be Real: Admit Past Indiscretions

One of the largest draws to a Public Relations Society of America meeting was the presentation, "My Favorite P.R. Failure." Six seasoned, highly respected pros in the field agreed to share a case study where something went awry. Chapter members, media, and guests flocked to the luncheon to laugh at someone else's mistakes.

While attendees need to know what to do to be a success, no one wants to look up to the speaker as a god. If all you can tout are your accomplishments, you make success look easy and a bit distant to mere mortals who daily battle life's challenges. You'll earn respect and admiration from the crowd if you candidly share mistakes you made along the way. With you serving as the fall guy, others can avoid those pitfalls and more quickly reach their goal. After all, if they wanted to make all those mistakes themselves, why would they attend your seminar or speech? They're paying you to share shortcuts to success, and they want to know how *not* to do something as much as *how* to do it. People want to hear personal stories, and if you can illustrate a point with a funny story, all the better.

Jeanine Just believes her success as a speaker is directly linked to the fact that her audiences sense that she is honest and genuine. "I wear my emotions on my sleeve," she says. "If I trip and fall walking up to the podium, we all stand there and laugh. People trust me when I speak. I have an open, easy style; I don't put myself up on a pedestal. I'm right there with the audience, talking about what is important to them and assisting them with issues they want to deal with."

Just says that her primary marketing objective is to build relationships. "I don't invest in Madison Avenue marketing techniques, but if I treat my audiences right, they will come back and refer me to others. You can't have a salesforce better than that."

Kent echoes the sentiment. "You must have a clear idea of who and what you are and be willing to be honest and admit your weaknesses if you want to win over an audience," he says. "Be prepared to talk about your topic, but don't have a prepared speech. The fewer formulas you use the better. And, as Shakespeare's Polonias said, 'Above all, to thy own self be true.'"

Conclude with a Call to Action

Last impressions are lasting. Don't kill the excitement you've created during your presentation with a weak ending. At all costs, avoid the phrase, "And in conclusion," and never apologize for your presentation. While thanking the group for having you is a nice gesture, it's not an ending that will win an Emmy.

If possible, save a particular pithy, thought-provoking quote to leave with the audience. Or wow them with your best joke. If you don't have material that will tickle their funny bone or tug at their heart strings, at least leave your audience with a summary of the main points of your speech, presented in a quick three-point fashion. Remember the adage, "Tell them what you'll tell them, tell them, and then tell them what you told them."

Don't wind up any speech without asking for the order. Hand out a brochure or pass out information on steps they can take to help overcome a problem or resolve a pressing issue. Then summarize verbally what they can do about a certain problem in an easy-to-follow three- or four-step plan.

No matter how you end, be sure to end on time. Use Henry's timer idea, take your watch off to remind yourself of the time limit, or ask the program chairperson or individual who hired you to stand when your time has run out. Then, in less than two minutes, wind up. Even if you have ten minutes more of material, it's better to leave the audience begging for more than to run on and make attendees excuse themselves while you are talking. Remember, how can they miss you when you won't go away?

Prepare for the dreaded question-and-answer session by planting a question or two in the audience ahead of time. Remember, few people like to go first, and most are certain that their questions will sound simple and that they shouldn't insult you and the others in the audience by asking. Once people start asking questions, repeat the question so that all can hear. If you don't know the answer, don't punt. Simply say you don't know.

And don't leave the seminar or speech site without your evaluations. These are invaluable tools for improving your presentation. Two questions beyond the obvious to consider are as follows:

1. What was the one point of value you gained from the workshop?

2. What will you do with the information? How can you use it?

Take the answers to the survey to heart, but don't be heartbroken if you don't always get rave reviews. Evaluate the opinions and don't look back, only ahead.

Before members of the audience leave, make sure each one of them has a brochure or a telephone index card that includes a few lines about your business and speech or seminar topics you offer. If they liked what you had to say, the chances of a referral are good if you make it easy for them to remember who you are.

They Know Who You Are, But Do You Know Who They Are?

Everyone who has attended your class, seminar, or speech knows who you are, and they know your background and how to get in touch with you from the class catalog or seminar brochure, your introduction, and handouts. Speaking opportunities give you a chance to put your name in front of small intimate groups and large impersonal audiences. But no matter what the size, it's easy for a speaker to walk away and not know the name of one person who heard him or her speak.

If you teach a class, keep a copy of the class roster that includes students' names and addresses. Then, stay in touch with those students at least once a year, either by sending handouts you think might be interesting or by holding a reunion. Each year, Henry invites a researcher to speak at his marketing class. At the end of the semester, he sends all of his former students an invitation to a potluck and update lecture by the researcher. The reunion gives former students a chance to network with others in the field, and it keeps Henry's name in front of an ever-growing number of people who may bring business to him.

If you're giving an hour-long speech at a luncheon or dinner meeting, you can get the names of attendees by having a drawing for a book that you've written or a tape that you've produced. Collect their business cards for a drawing. A week or two later, send each attendee a handout related to the speech topic and accompanied by a personal "FYI" note. Henry earned a million-dollar account from a former student with whom he kept in touch in just this way.

When your speech or class has concluded, write down pertinent information that will help you with future presentations to the same group. Lee S. Shapiro, J. D., is nationally known as the "Hugging" Judge and for his powerful talks on human relations. After each presentation, Shapiro fills out an After-Presentation Reference Sheet that includes

name, address, and phone number of the organization
name and phone number of the contact person
type of meeting
title of presentation
number of attendees
type of attendees
room set-up
things to prepare for next time
distance from airport

When a company or organization asks Shapiro for an encore, he's prepared, and he ensures that his repeat performances live up to and even surpass his initial presentation.

To learn more about how the pros do it, consider attending events sponsored by the National Speakers Association (NSA) or joining this group of over 3,000 members. Many cities offer local NSA chapters, and the association holds a number of national conventions each year. For information, call or write: NSA, 3877 North 7th St. #350, Phoenix, Arizona, 85014, (602) 265-1001.

Top Self-Marketing Secrets
Pointers for the Platform

1. Practice makes perfect. Put yourself in front of a live audience of friends to get honest feedback about your information and speaking style.

2. Begin by giving talks to college classes and teaching for university extended studies programs.

3. Tie in to your local chamber of commerce.

4. Sponsor your own seminar.

5. Distribute a speakers' bureau brochure to professional organizations and corporations.

6. Research the audience to ensure that your talk meets their needs.

7. Create an opening act that sizzles.

8. Use fill-in-the-blanks handouts and other visual aids such as slides, overhead transparencies, and videos to keep the audience awake.

9. Reward participation to involve the audience.

10. Stop talking when the buzzer sounds.

11. Get business cards or class rosters for follow-up marketing.

12. Distribute speaker evaluations.

13. Charge for your talent when appropriate.

9

It's Better to Give
So You'll Receive
Faith and Hope Are Nice,
But Charity Gets Coverage

Hitching your wagon to a worthy cause lets you give back to the community that supports you. It will also earn you a reputation as a businessperson who cares about more than the bottom line. Although few go into a pro bono endeavor (pro bono publico—for the good of the public) for the sole purpose of building clientele, when pressed, many businesspeople agree that it is a way to expand contacts, to earn referrals, and to broaden your experience without the self-serving hype of blatant marketing approaches.

Kevin Alverson, national anesthesiology account manager for Northern Health Systems, Inc., joined with close friend Kyle Eldred to create Critical Mass, a nonprofit group of young professionals who get together on a regular basis to organize fund-raisers for a local children's charity. "We had a group of friends who would each pitch in $100 to throw a party that 400-500 people would attend. One day while walking down the beach, Kyle and I decided that if we could get half of that crowd to attend a $75-a-plate black-tie affair, we could donate a sizable sum to a community group and take our party to another level."

The first year, the twosome approached the Big Brothers and Big Sisters organizations. "We told them that all they had to do was let us use their name and we would donate the proceeds to them," explains Alverson. "Many board members were familiar with my work as a Big Brother, but they still put us through an hour of questioning. They were suspicious at first as to why two young professionals on the fast track would do something out of the ordinary like this. We convinced them that a smile on a child's face was what we were looking for."

The Big Brothers organization made Alverson and Eldred sign a contract holding the two personally responsible for the event. They rallied together with fourteen other Pittsburgh professionals and raised $3,400 for the charity. By the second year, Critical Mass raised $12,000 for the Make a Wish Foundation, and the third year another $12,000 for Special Olympics.

In addition to helping kids in the community, Kevin's big heart has helped him to gain professionally and personally. "I've made a lot of contacts including ex-Steelers Lynn Swan and Franco Harris," says Alverson. "I've also met the local hosts of 'PM Magazine,' who have, in turn, invited us to some big fund-raisers where we've met the mayor and other politically involved people."

Workwise, write-ups in his corporation's newsletter about the efforts of Critical Mass helped him earn a favorable reputation among people in site offices whom he had never met. "When I went to a national sales convention and met a man who recognized me from a newsletter article, he immediately perceived me not only as a good sales rep, but as someone who can step back from work and be successful in other endeavors."

Alverson also credits landing a new job to his charity work. "The president of the company at which I'm now working was at the second black and white ball we threw and approached me to talk about this job. The organization, caliber, and outcome of the event impressed him. When I landed the job, he authorized a contract that states that I am allowed unlimited 'comp' time to devote to Critical Mass. He takes pride in what I do. And since I'm his employee, he knows that he is himself contributing to the success of the event."

Today, Critical Mass is thirty-five members strong. Charities now approach it to be considered the recipient of their annual fund-raising parties. "Once you are involved in a charity, you realize that no matter how rough a day you have, there is always someone having a worse time. It's a great way to channel energies and a phenomenal way to help you grow."

Kevin gives one caveat: "Don't go into charity work to use it as a résumé filler. You'll stand out like a sore thumb and you won't get anything out of it. Do it for self-growth and to give of yourself, and you'll gain the world."

James B. Strenski, Public Relations Society of America (PRSA) fellow, chairman of Public Communications Inc., with offices in Chicago, Miami, and Tampa, echoes the sentiment. James donates 20 percent of his time to pro bono initiatives. "Our company feels strongly that we owe the community and the professions we are a part of a certain amount of our time," he says. "Our attitude is much like the character in *The Magnificent Obsession*—we take whatever chance we have to do something for someone else, without asking for anything in return."

Strenski has risen through the ranks of his professional organization, having held national offices for the society and serving for two years as chair of the Public Service Committee. "The payback has been meeting colleagues who operate public relations firms throughout the United States, Canada, and even offshore," he says. "They have become good friends, as well as sources of business referrals. Our association also gave rise to the formation of the Worldcom Group, Inc., a partnership organization of corporate financial marketing and institutional communication public relations agencies to share resources as well as referrals."

When Strenski chaired the marketing committee of Tampa Downtown Partnership, a private businessperson's group dedicated to economic development of downtown Tampa, he expected to give time and direction. The group's efforts resulted in the city's providing funding for marketing, and Strenski's firm was selected because of its volunteer leadership.

It's no secret that volunteerism gives as much to the person who donates the time, money, and energy as it does to the recipient. So while you don't go into pro bono work looking to get something out of it, there is nothing deceptive about volunteering to help promote or support a venture that also gives your business or product notoriety. You can bet that celebrities who sing for Farm Aid or stand up to fight against environmental concerns benefit from the goodwill of their names' association with the cause.

Earn Visibility As a Board Member

One of the most direct ways to meet key industry leaders is to sit on a board of directors of a community-based organization. A seat on a board of directors is a position of prestige you have to earn. But when your hard work and expertise precede you, you will begin to be asked to sit on boards to direct the efforts of philanthropic or nonprofit organizations. Everything you've done to date—speaking, writing, volunteering—creates the momentum of compounding interest until suddenly, after years of investing, the payback is big.

Dick Daniels and Jack Berkman, partners in Berkman & Daniels, a San Diego marketing–communications firm, have given their time serving on the boards of the San Diego Symphony Association, the San Diego Repertory Theater, the San Diego Press Club, the Century Club, the Reuben H. Fleet Space and Science Foundation, the San Diego-Imperial County Chapter of the March of Dimes Birth Defects Foundation, and the Foundation's National Council of Volunteers.

"This pro bono work keeps us directly in touch with many of the important publics our clients must deal with," says Berkman. "And it gives us a good feeling, in terms of service to the community in which our business operates."

But don't think you have to wait patiently to be asked to join a board. Many organizations welcome volunteers for these positions. The American Cancer Society, for example, has numerous boards with positions just waiting for qualified, industrious individuals. Whether it's a graphic artist, marketing representative, or printer who volunteers for the marketing communications board or a banker, stockbroker, or attorney who is available for the planned-giving board, there are opportunities just right for you if you let your desires be known.

Every step you take to become more visible is one step closer to the next contact and the next deal. Some days you may wonder why you're leaving work early for yet another meeting or why you're taking time to raise money for a charity when your own business seems like a philanthropic effort. But tomorrow the payoff will come via a person who knew a person who recommended you. Actual clients or customers may not know exactly why they came to you or how they got your name, but they *will* know that they have heard of you and that everyone they asked for a referral listed your name among the top. All of the effort, all of the visibility, and all of the selfless giving comes back in spades. (It's like tithing. Once you make the commitment to give, you somehow "find" the resources. And the more you give, the more you receive.)

If You Give It Away, Will You Get It Back?

You're asked to do a freebie. You don't have the time. You are reluctant to spend potentially billable hours without being paid. Should you carve time out of nights and weekends to do nonprofit work? Most likely the answer is yes, if

- The person who is asking is important to you.
- You are not being taken advantage of.
- Your name will get out among others who could be potential clients.
- You'll have an opportunity to meet key contacts.
- You want to prove your talents and capabilities to the organization to earn future business.
- You simply get a warm, fuzzy feeling by doing it.
- It will be a worthwhile addition to your résumé or portfolio.
- Your present clients and customers won't suffer from lack of attention.

When coauthor Diane donated close to fifty hours writing a public relations plan and press kit that included fact sheets, bios, and news releases for the first San Diego Women's Business Grant, she knew the contacts with top female entrepreneurs would be beneficial. But when, she wondered, would she be able to point to positive cash flow as a direct result of the effort? Two days after the grant luncheon, a woman who had seen her name and photo in the event program and had seen Diane stand up during introductions, called for an appointment. The next month, Diane's firm began providing public relations services for the woman's company.

For four years Jeff Harper, president of Capitol Communications and vice president of the Canzeri Company, a full-service public relations and events firm in Washington, D.C., donated his services to coordinate and produce the Nancy Reagan Annual Tennis Tournament for the "Just Say No" campaign. "Being associated with that event was without a doubt a good marketing tool for us," says Harper. "Working with the Reagans for four years certainly helped build our credibility when pitching other accounts. You have to be visible in Washington. And the more you are out there—pro bono or not—the greater the potential for business."

After the Reagans left town, Harper became involved in putting together the "Dan Quayle Tennis Challenge" to benefit the Leukemia Society, a corporate sponsor-driven event. "How an effort will translate into business later on is hard to tell; but those who attend always want to know who did what," says Harper. "We do a lot of volunteer work because we believe we should. If we're lucky, we can make some new contacts, and inevitably there is a possible spin-off for the agency."

But Harper does caution enthusiastic volunteers, "Don't forget which side your bread is buttered on. It doesn't behoove you to donate an unrealistic amount of time to charity if your paying customers don't get the attention they expect." Take volunteer positions seriously, but don't overcommit.

Banking on the Ripple Effect

Leigh Steinberg, one of the country's most successful sports agents, makes sure that he donates money and time to each one of his clients' charity causes. Part of his goal in doing so is to help undo the typical stereotype of the sports agent as a sleazy salesman. In the May 1989 issue of *Continental Profiles*, author Neil Choen quoted Steinberg as saying, "...[Athletes] really need to develop long-term relationships in a city or a community that will transcend that short sports career. So the responsible thing to do also has opportunities for them. They're meeting businessmen and other people across the community, and when their careers end, those relationships are there in terms of second-career opportunities."

It's the spin-off and ripple effect of involvement in charitable causes that Steinberg impresses upon his clients as being important. Steinberg helped to develop former San Diego Charger Rolf Benirschke's "Kicks for Critters," in which the field goal kicker would donate money to the San Diego Zoo's fund for endangered species every time he made a field goal. The football player then put together a board of directors of leading figures in local politics, business, and the media to support a campaign that asked the public to match Benirschke's pledges at any level—from a nickel to a dollar per field goal. The program raised more than $1 million for the fund and immeasurably elevated Benirschke's status and prestige in the community and the nation.

Is It Worth Trading Services?

Bartering your services won't cover the overhead, but it might earn new business that can lead to fully paid accounts. Don't shy away from a trade, especially if it gives you the opportunity to get experience in a new field, to receive special recognition, or to meet movers and shakers.

When George Chanos approached Diane and asked her company to provide public relations services in exchange for sweat equity in his new board game, Notable Quotables, the offer intrigued her. Chanos dangled the success that Trivial Pursuit sweat equity partners enjoyed in front of her like a diamond carat.

But Diane knew she couldn't put two or three account executives on the job with only a promise of future income. Owning a share of a potentially big-selling game was exciting. After all, Trivial Pursuit earned $6.5 million in the first year—that's more than it would cost to buy Eastern Airlines. After much discussion, Diane and George came to an agreement. The Gage Group would cut its hourly fee in half when it worked on the game project, receiving 50 percent of its earnings in cash. The other 50 percent would go toward buying shares of the game.

In the meantime, the Gage Group, which up to this time had primarily promoted services, gained experience it didn't have publicizing a consumer product. It made key media contacts with reporters who became excited about the local invention, and it earned the public relations company credibility promoting a new product. In turn, Chanos got top-notch public relations services for half the price.

Another way to barter services and to get free ad space is to learn of upcoming trade fairs, conferences, seminars, and other special events at which you would like to be represented. There may be a service you can provide the event planners in exchange for the opportunity to get in front of the audience either as a guest speaker or as a vendor displaying your product or touting your services. You don't always have to pay for self-promotion in cold hard cash.

Sponsorships Gain You a Different Kind of Visibility

Sponsoring a charity event to earn visibility is something the big guys have done for years. Whether it's a golf or tennis tournament, 10K run or marathon, art exhibition, or wine-tasting party, charitable causes are always looking for business sponsors.

Tying your name in with a particular event or cause can get your name out to new audiences in a non-self-serving way. Jack-in-the-Box restaurants, owned by Food Maker, Inc., created a "Put the Bite on Literacy" campaign in which it asked people to bring in used books to its restaurants. When customers complied, they'd receive a discount coupon on a particular food item. Jack-in-the-Box then held a book sale and auction at one of its stores, donating proceeds to the Council on Literacy. Of course, the food chain made free Jack-in-the-Box food available at the event to win more converts.

Reebok International has won many hearts *and* feet with its Human Rights Awards. For several years it has recognized individuals who have worked for human rights at an annual presentation. The commitment has been expensive, but it has raised the company's profile and earned numerous admirers and media coverage that can't be bought. It's estimated that more than

570 million United States consumers read about the second award ceremony, which featured rock star Sting and ex-president Jimmy Carter as speakers and gave awards to Chinese students, tribal peoples of the Malaysian rain forests, relatives of the "disappeared" in Argentina, and Americans who helped the plight of Native Americans. *USA Today*, the *Washington Post*, MTV, "Entertainment Tonight," CNN, and all major footwear magazines covered the event. A video news release (a prepackaged taped story on the event) aired on sixty-two stations nationwide, capturing more than 1.6 million viewers. Charity can pay big dividends.

You don't have to be a mega-corporation to help others and to earn recognition for it. The San Diego Chapter of the American Marketing Association won hearts when it created a Community Services Committee to provide professional marketing guidance to area nonprofit organizations. The first year it named the Women's Resource Center as beneficiary; it helped design a logo and promotional materials for its new family shelter, as well as communication pieces for fund-raising events. The association contributed its talent and earned local visibility for its generosity. Ask yourself what resources you can offer to a community group or organization. Here are a few examples:

- A new restaurant throws a grand-opening party with all proceeds benefiting a hospital auxiliary.

- A clothing boutique offers the latest styles for a fashion show fund-raiser.

- A bookstore sponsors a book-signing party to raise money for a special-interest group.

- Attorneys offer a day of free telephone legal counseling for a law school fund-raiser.

- An image consultant agrees to provide free holiday hair and makeup services for cancer patients at a local hospital.

- A physician group volunteers time at a community health fair.

Advertising Your Charity Tie-ins— Don't Keep Them a Secret

Don't keep your benevolence to yourself. If you're doing something worthwhile, let your customers, clients, and potential supporters know. If you're a cosponsor of an event, be sure that your logo gets on the program or entry form. Ask for signage at the event or a free booth where you can display your wares or give away samples.

Paid advertising touting your involvement can be a wise investment of your dollars. General Dynamics, an aerospace giant, took out a full-page magazine ad describing a program it sponsors that involves women prisoners in a work program to revitalize a neighborhood. The women learn new skills—carpentry, dry wall hanging, roofing—and gain confidence. The community gets high-quality, affordable housing. General Dynamics gets its name and tag line—"General Dynamics, a Strong Company for a Strong Country"—in front of readers and it positions itself as a valuable community citizen.

Likewise, Ford Motor Company bought a full-page to advertise the Ford Motor Company Collection at the Metropolitan Museum of Art. Prominent at the bottom of the ad is the Ford logo and tag line, "Ford Motor Company takes you farther than ever before."

MasterCard also advertised its "Choose to Make a Difference" program in which it offered consumers the choice of a charitable cause to which MasterCard would donate money. Every time a consumer used his or her card or bought MasterCard Travelers Cheques in a certain time frame, the company would make a contribution to the specified fund. The ad included a "ballot" that the customer filled out and sent in indicating his or her choice of one of six charities. Wouldn't you pull out that charge card over another if you knew you could be making a charitable contribution at the same time? That's what MasterCard was banking on.

Grabbing Media Attention with Freebies

Charity does get coverage, especially when what you do is offbeat, whimsical, touching, or involves animals or children.

As Christmas 1990 approached and American soldiers were in the midst of Operation Desert Shield, a postal service company offered to send packages to the Middle East at no charge. It received a week of free media exposure and immeasurable goodwill. That kind of gift isn't fast forgotten.

Shortly after Halloween, one business collected pumpkins that would otherwise rot and donated them to a zoo for animals to eat. The report, picked up on the wire service, spread throughout the country as a fun day-after-Halloween story.

Apple Computers made an indelible mark on American homes when it donated computers to schools throughout the nation. While the effort was no doubt generous, you can bet Apple liked the fact that school kids everywhere were learning computer skills on its hardware and becoming entrenched in the Apple system.

Sometimes, the more offbeat your effort, the better chance of coverage. A public relations–advertising man, Gary Beals, earned his company recognition when he became administrator of the newly revived San Diego Hell on Earth Club. This tongue-in-cheek venture alerted potential newcomers to the city's pitfalls—earthquakes, smog, astronomical real estate prices, and the like—in the hope that they wouldn't move to the area. Three large photos of Beals in action promoting the club and an accompanying story ran in all editions of the *Los Angeles Times*. Of course, the story mentioned Gary's advertising agency, and he was also interviewed on National Public Radio, which showed listeners that he has a way of earning media coverage.

Increasing Media Opportunities

An added bonus of working for a nonprofit organization is that you'll get media coverage you never would otherwise. While your venture on its own may be too commercial, when you tie in with a charity, your name will appear in public service announcements (PSAs) and other blurbs about the event.

Radio and television PSAs are scarcer and scarcer, but if your event is truly worthwhile and benefits a charity, your chances for "free" air time are greater. Be sure to send PSAs to radio stations at least two weeks prior to the time you want coverage to begin. Thus, if you'd like mention on the air for the two weeks prior to the event, the PSA needs to be at the station a month ahead of time.

Send written, not taped, PSAs to radio so that the disk jockeys can read them over the air. Type the PSAs one to a page and time them for ten, twenty, or thirty seconds. Using a sixty-five-space line, ten seconds is two-and-one-half lines. Time yourself reading the PSA at a moderate pace and shorten it until you're on the money.

Television stations also accept PSAs but use them much less frequently than they did before the FCC bowed out of becoming a watchdog of public programming in the late 1970s. One of the best ways to get the attention of a television station is to get a station reporter or anchor to take part in your event. If a television personality is the honorary chairperson or emcee for the event, the TV station will more likely tape a PSA using its on-air talent. It makes the station look good in the eyes of the community, and it gets its name out in a positive way to its audience.

To recruit a television personality, either write a letter to the person or contact the station's public affairs department. Be very clear about what will be expected of the person, and don't demand too much. Lending his or her name and making opening remarks or a quick speech is all that should be expected. If possible, send background information about the event so that the television celebrity gets a feel for how it benefits the charity or community.

Society editors at newspapers are on the lookout to cover events with pizazz. If you're hosting a party, be sure to send the media special invitations, and do it as far in advance as possible, since their calendars get booked quickly.

Publicize your nonprofit event by sending calendar items to the local newspapers and magazines as well. If possible, give monthly periodicals a three-month lead time, weeklies a month, and dailies at least two weeks. If your name can be tagged onto the name of the event, all the better. You'll be mentioned every time an item is run. If not, realize that gaining publicity for the event eventually works in your favor because the more people who attend, the more who will become familiar with your services.

No matter how you donate your services to charity, be a cheerful giver. And don't shortchange yourself or the philanthropic effort by doing things halfway because you're not getting paid. You can win referrals if you first win hearts. Give it your all or don't give at all.

Top Self-Marketing Secrets

Give and You'll Receive

1. Serve on charities to gain notoriety, but don't go into pro bono work solely as a résumé filler.

2. Become active in your professional organization to earn sources of business referrals.

3. Don't wait patiently for a board position—volunteer.

4. Volunteering is like tithing. The more you give, the more you receive.

5. Look for the ripple effect—the client who got your name from a number of referrals—to prove that your philanthropic efforts are paying off.

6. Use volunteerism to build credibility when pitching new accounts.

7. Trade services as a way to earn experience in a new field.

8. Barter your expertise with trade shows and conferences in exchange for an opportunity to speak or to display as a vendor.

9. Sponsor an event with proceeds benefiting a charity.

10. Don't keep your benevolence a secret. Let your customers and potential supporters know when you're doing something worthwhile.

11. Create a publicity stunt for a charity, the more offbeat the better.

12. Win public service announcements by recruiting a radio or TV personality as the honorary chair of a charitable event.

10

How to Win Friends and Influence Referrals
Love Letters Straight from the Start

We are here to challenge conventional wisdom. It is easy to make fun of the post office. One joke says that half the price of a stamp is for delivery and the other half is for storage. But we say postage stamps are the biggest bargain in America.

For an investment of only a few cents, you can give a priceless gift: a few words of praise. In the 1830s, the writings of English educator, Rowland Hill, convinced the United States and British governments that volume was the key to a cheap postal system. For his brilliance, he was named Sir Rowland, and when he died they buried him in Westminster Abbey. While in Sir Rowland's day the United States Postal Service handled six pieces of mail per year per citizen, by the late 1970s that average had climbed to 427. Today, the United States Post Office handles 166.3 billion pieces of mail per year—almost half as much as the rest of the world combined.

Are you sending your fair share of mail to valued suppliers, vendors, and potential referral sources? We all treasure personal mail that makes us feel good. By employing this truth—and our cheap postal service—you can do wonders for your business.

The Greatest Thanks You Can Give

With our frantically busy lifestyles, we often don't take the time to say thank you properly. Investing the time it takes to do so can give your business an extra edge.

One professional who can attest to the power of a good thank you letter is Gale Tobin. Today president of her own advertising agency, Tobin recalls a time when she worked at a large agency as an account executive. It was then she learned what a prized possession a thank-you letter can be.

One of Tobin's clients was a home builder who was introducing a new community on a tight time frame. Her job was to produce a full-color brochure in less than a week for a VIP preview reception. Not only would all of the executives from Tobin's client be on hand, but the president and top management from the firm's parent company were flying in for the event.

Tobin's dilemma is one we all face in business. Only part of the project rested in her control. A large part laid in someone else's domain, namely the printer. Have you seen the cartoon most printers have in their lobbies? Four nebbish cartoon characters are laughing heartily under the caption "You want it when?"

But Tobin had a good relationship with her printing representative, John Woodrow, who went the extra mile. He rallied the printing crew to put in overtime. As soon as he could get a partial batch, he loaded enough brochures into his car and drove them through rush-hour traffic. The brochures arrived with ten minutes to spare before the VIP reception.

Woodrow made Tobin a hero. But she knew it would not be the last time a rush printing job would be needed. So Tobin gave Woodrow a gift money can't buy: sincere praise. She did it with a letter from her boss, the president of the agency, to Woodrow's boss at the print shop.

Although the letter was not long, it was powerful. It said that finding star employees was not easy, and the company should feel fortunate to have John Woodrow because he is a star. The letter thanked the entire printing crew for coming through when it really counted. In closing, it said, "We were so impressed with John's performance, we are taking the liberty of sending him a copy of this letter."

How would you feel if you received this letter about one of your employees? And how would you feel if you were the employee being bragged about to your boss? In this instance, the printer sent a thank you letter back to the agency that was twice the length of the one it received. The agency's letter had been placed on a bulletin board for all the employees to read. The printer said it was the first time in the company's history that it had received such a letter of genuine thanks.

Which raises another question. If ever there is another rush job, do you think the printing company will come through for the agency? If the printer was asked to give a recommendation for an ad agency, you can also be sure Tobin's firm would be at the top of their list.

Letters Bring You Lagniappe

It is amazing at how few people take the time to give another company sincere praise. Coauthor Henry learned this when he produced a radio commercial using three nationally known entertainers in Hollywood. Although Henry had made many local commercials, it was his first experience directing the acting talents of big stars. A lot was riding on the spot's success. Henry had not only talked his client into spending a bunch of money on a radio campaign, but he also sold them on the extra expense of doing the commercial in Hollywood with three recognizable television and film stars.

One of the star's agents recommended a recording studio called Sound Advice as a good place to do the spot. Located near the legendary intersection of Hollywood and Vine, the Sound Advice lobby was lined with awards for creative excellence. Henry found out why. Despite their being less than ten years out of college, the firm's principals, Lou Schwing and Matt Wright, were very good at the touchy job of directing stars with decades of acting experience. Schwing and Wright coaxed take after take from the stars, until the final commercial was perfect. The real test came when the commercial aired. As they say in the ad game, the commercial made turnstiles turn and cash registers ring. Henry sent a letter of praise that said more than thanks. The letter said that the commercial they recorded helped his client enjoy the best first quarter sales in company history.

The morning that the Sound Advice partners opened the letter, Henry received a phone call. Despite the many awards, it was their first unsolicited testimonial. When asked if they could use it to show new clients, Henry told them that was exactly why he had sent it.

On future projects with Sound Advice, Henry always received what the shopkeepers in New Orleans call lagniappe—a little something extra. When you order a dozen pecan praline candies and the shopkeeper gives you thirteen, that is lagniappe. If you are extra nice to the counter help at the ice cream parlor and you notice your scoop of ice cream is bigger than the other customers', that too is lagniappe. Once the studio redid a commercial on its own initiative because it thought it could do a better job with the sound effects. Later Sound Advice even solved what could have been an ugly situation for Henry with AFTRA, the performers union, on a project that did not concern them. And they did not charge him for their time. Now that's really lagniappe.

Finding and building strong bonds with key groups will help your firm grow and thrive. The letter to Sound Advice is an example of an overlooked part of marketing for professionals. It lets you get that little something extra when you really need it. Sincere praise through the mail is a great way to make this happen.

Your letters are not manipulation. For the strategy to work, you must be sincere in your praise. The overall concept is stated best in Dale Carnegie training and in his classic book, *How to Win Friends and Influence People.* If you have not read the book, it should be a must for the coming year.

Use Letters to Inspire Others to Greatness

Think about those with whom you do business who help you succeed. Your job does not end when you locate good assistance. It's one thing to contract with good people, but it is quite another to inspire them do their best.

A few professionals take a hard-nosed, overly demanding approach with the vendors they hire, much like a football coach or a Marine drill instructor. Their rationale being that you get only what you demand. But in truth, this is really counterproductive with creative people and only serves to alienate them. The authors have found that where some measure of creativity is involved, vendors will deal with the overly demanding approach in one of two ways: they let work linger, or they whip it out as rapidly as possible in order to do projects for those they like to work with. Either scenario is bad for you. If you feel you are not getting the service you deserve from vendors, better to replace them than to bully them. Demands just don't work.

If you like something, say so. Most professionals hear news only when it is bad. An occasional word of praise can spur them to produce even better work. Even when you want the project reworked, begin by praising what you liked about it. This will soften the blow when you tell them what's wrong. Always try to frame the bad news with good news. For your sake, you want them in a positive frame of mind when they return to your project. But always try to praise more often than you criticize. A few kind words are a powerful reward. What gets rewarded, gets repeated.

Please Note: A Quickie Letter-Writing Checklist

Here is a quick checklist on how to write letters that will win friends and influence referrals.

1. Write the letter to someone your contact wants to impress. If it's an employee, send the letter to the boss. If the person is self-employed, write a letter that will impress potential clients.

2. Tell exactly how your contact made cash registers ring. Specific figures carry more weight than generalities. Mention numbers like net savings—sales percentage increases or total volume.

3. Say how that person's efforts made you feel. Were you proud, relieved or impressed? Tell him or her.

4. Call the person a star.

5. Keep the letter short. Many people are afraid to write a long letter because it will take too much time or mental energy. So they put it aside for later. But a short letter can be done quickly.

Here is a sample letter to show you what we mean.

```
Gail Conwell
Gail Conwell Design
13684 Boquita Drive
Del Mar, CA 92014
```

Dear Gail:

You are a star designer. The magazine ad you prepared for our parenting information hotline was the most successful in our history.

More than 800 calls were received the week the ad appeared. That really made us feel good that we could be helping that many new moms and dads.

You are a pleasure to work with. You care about creating excellent ads and are willing to go the extra mile.

Thank you again for a job well done. If you ever need a good reference for a prospective client, please have them give me a call.

Sincerely,

```
The Independent Order of Foresters
Henry J. DeVries
Director of Communications
```

Try Saying Thank You in Advance

If you hired someone to do a task that is really important to you, try saying thank you in advance. Suppose you are on trial for first-degree murder and you have hired the best attorney you could find. You are innocent, of course, but if your lawyer can't convince the jury of that, you are headed for the gas chamber. But first you'll get to enjoy living with a new roommate who was already convicted of murder.

Here is our recommendation if this happens to you. Buy your attorney a nice gift. Send the gift with a letter of praise that explains why you selected this attorney. If your attorney has a boss, by all means send that person a copy of the letter. Now answer this question. Do you think your attorney might work a little harder for you?

Don't wait until your life is at stake to try this. Henry did it when he organized a disaster relief effort for the Independent Order of Foresters following the devastating San Francisco earthquake. Within seventy-two hours he was on the scene trying to locate members of this fraternal group who needed assistance.

Since phone communications were severely limited, Henry decided to print a flyer for delivery to shelters to offer assistance to IOF members. When he went to a print shop and asked for the flyers by 2 P.M. the next afternoon, he was told it was impossible. The print shop was a mess since the quake. Jobs were backed up. They were short staffed. Maybe he could have it by 6 P.M., but it would probably be the next day. Many people would try to demand that the work be done faster, but Henry tried a different strategy.

A few doors down from the print shop was a bakery. Its specialty was extra-thick, extra-chewy chocolate chip cookies with large chunks of chocolate. Henry bought a dozen of the cookies and took them back to the print shop. He attached a note that said: "Thank you in advance for your hard work. Here is some energy food to keep you going during these hectic days. I know you'll finish my flyer for the earthquake victims as soon as you can."

Guess what? The most amazing thing happened. Not only was the job done the next day, it was finished by 9 A.M. That was twenty-four hours ahead of schedule. The cookies and the note were prominently displayed in the print shop. Now whose print job do you think they did first? That of the person who threw his weight around, or the guy who gave them those big, chewy chocolate chip cookies?

We all are human beings, and we all love appreciation. Motivational speaker Jim Rohn often discusses this topic. Rohn says if we want better service, we need to find more clever ways to spend our money. One clever way is to bring back the true notion of tips, which originated as money given waiters in advance. Tips is really an acronym for "To Insure Prompt Service." If you really want to impress some lunch friends, give the waitress ten dollars before the meal. Tell her you really want your guests well taken care of. "She won't only give you great service, she'll hover," says Rohn.

Now we don't recommend slipping a five-dollar-bill to your defense attorney or architect, but the same principle holds true. An appropriate gift and a few written words of praise that others can see will work wonders. People treat others like they are treated.

Keep the Cards and Letters Coming

Don't stop with thank you letters. Think of other ways you can use the mail to further your business. Here are a baker's dozen of ideas that will make you remembered.

1. Give your clients a copy of this book. Maybe they will read this chapter and give you a great testimonial letter.

2. When clients call to thank you on the phone, ask them if they would be kind enough to put it in writing. If you don't ask, you don't get. About half will send you a letter. Copies of testimonial letters make great additions to proposals to prospective clients.

3. Sometimes letters from particular clients would be very valuable. Don't wait for them to call, call them. Tell them why you want it and that you would be happy to send them a rough draft.

4. If you are involved in a worthwhile community project, ask government officials for a letter of endorsement. Henry has done this successfully with the White House, various state governors, and local mayors.

5. When you see a magazine article a client might be interested in, clip it and send it to him. Articles that pertain to business are great, but don't forget articles that would be of personal interest. Maybe it is about the client's college alma mater, hometown, or favorite hobby.

6. When you travel, send postcards to clients, suppliers, vendors, and others you want to form linkages with. But don't send a long-winded "Having a wonderful time...hope everything's fine," message. A postcard is just to say you are thinking of them. So instead, send a quip or short observation. Here are some of our favorites.

   - "We came. We saw. We bought souvenirs."
   - "Yesterday in Florida had alligator for lunch. Which is better than the other way around."
   - "We spent a week here one night."
   - "In this town women wear insect repellant instead of perfume."
   - "This town is so small the grocery store puts Velveeta in the gourmet food section."

7. Here's another postcard idea. Before you leave on your trip, type the names and addresses on a sheet of mail labels. Then you can just peel off the address. Sending postcards doesn't have to be time consuming. Also, remember to buy a sheet of postcard stamps before you go.

8. Clip funny cartoons and news items from the newspaper. The gift of laughter can go a long way.

9. Here is a better idea than flowers for someone who is hospitalized. Buy a stack of get-well cards. Each day the person is in the hospital or at home recuperating, send a card. You might send anywhere from seven to two dozen. Save a nice note for the last one. Say that, from now on, the person should be well on the road to recovery.

10. Think twice before you send clients cards on their birthdays or for the holidays. You can make a better impression if you send cards to their children who are twelve and under. Kids love mail. And parents fondly remember someone who took the time to make their children happy.

11. Yet another postcard idea. Send the children postcards from the road. A one-page letter on hotel stationery also can be a thrill for a child.

12. Few things are as difficult as convincing big companies to pay small ones in less than thirty days. But the forces at the Gage Group, coauthor Diane's company, pushed through the bureaucratic maze by calling the accounting clerk at a large hospital to determine where their payment was in the cycle. They then followed up by sending thank you flowers in advance. The stunned accounting clerk was so taken aback that she showed the flowers and the note of praise to her boss. The next month, a new clerk was in the position (we like to think the old one got a promotion and raise) and he kiddingly joked that he liked candy. The next day a box of See's candy greeted him at work. The Gage Group's check was cut in record time.

13. A final idea from Anne Boe, a keynote motivational speaker and author of *Is Your "Net" Working?* Boe suggests the following. The next time a newspaper prints a nice feature article about you, take it to a print shop. Have them create a reprint that looks like a newsletter. Then mail it to potential clients and those you want to stay in touch with. Boe did this with a recent profile of hers in the *San Diego Business Journal.* She received several new client assignments when they received her "newsletter."

June 28, 1985

Henry J. DeVries
Roni Hicks Advertising and Public Relations
3170 Fourth Avenue, Suite 200
San Diego, CA 92103

Dear Henry:

On behalf of American Medical International, I would like to thank you most kindly for the role you played in making the North Coast Health Center/AMI a successful event. This groundbreaking set some very high standards for AMI.

Thank you most kindly for your creative thoughts, follow through, and management. We could not have done it without you.

I look forward to working with you in the future.

Sincerely yours,

Frank J. Kruntorad
Director of Marketing
American Medical International

FJK/tb

August 14, 1984

Ms. Jan Percival
Ms. Roni Hicks
Roni Hicks & Associates
2251 San Diego Avenue
Suite B-251
San Diego, CA 92110

Dear Jan and Roni,

Just a note of appreciation for the kind of public relations we have been receiving in the last 30 to 45 days. I appreciate you sending a folder monthly of all of our clippings and activities and wondered if that is going to be your policy on a continued basis. I cycle the folder throughout the organization so the balance of the people around here can see what you are doing. As far as I am concerned, you are doing an excellent job! I realize you had a Chapter 11 to work with and I wouldn't want to give you one of those each month, but, we are getting coverage and it's starting to be the talk of the town. Every place I go, people say "you rose from the dead."

Keep up the good work as we need the exposure and it builds confidence in our investors. The phones are ringing off the hook!

Again, thanks for your time and the quiet, very professional way in which you go about getting the job done.

Sincerely,

The Huffman Companies
Ray L. Huffman
President

April 1, 1987

Henry DeVries
Roni Hicks & Associates
3170 Fourth Avenue, Suite 200
San Diego, CA 92103

Dear Henry:

Just a note to let you know that the direct mail
letter you penned for me is getting results!

We had immediate response from Bureau members who
want to participate in our Passport San Diego
program. In fact, we have received response cards
every day for the past two weeks.

Mary Batten, our Membership Director, plans to
use your letter as a model for her future direct
mail pieces.

We truly appreciate your time and talents to
further this worthwhile project.

Very sincerely,

Dal L. Watkins
President
San Diego Convention & Visitors Bureau

DLW/sah

Top Self-Marketing Secrets

Tips to Win Friends and Influence Referrals through the Mail

1. Send thank yous to the boss of the person you want to thank. Call the person a star.

2. Say thank you in advance. A small investment in a thoughtful gift can reap a big return.

3. Don't stop with thank you letters. Keep notes and clippings coming so valuable contacts won't forget you.

4. Remember the humble postcard. Keep the message short and be funny if you can.

5. Kids love mail. Clients and contacts fondly remember someone who took the time to make a child feel special.

11

Guaranteed Better Letters or Your Money Back
Nine Sales Letter Secrets for the Nineties

Martin Thompson knew he needed marketing help. And he needed it now. Long before America had heard of television's Laura Palmer, Agent Cooper, or the log lady, Thompson founded a firm called Twin Peaks Pool Service—named after the area where he lived. The only mystery Thompson had to solve was how to find customers faster than you could say "pass the coffee and donuts."

After a successful ten-year career with a large hardware retailer, Thompson decided to step out of the corporate world. He went to work for a friend's pool cleaning business as an intermediate step before opening a pool service of his own. Soon after he learned the trade, his friend was forced to cut back. Overnight Thompson became a self-employed businessman, one with no clients and no prospects. The timing couldn't be worse. Thompson had just purchased a new home for his wife and toddler son, and the family was still trying to adjust to the bigger house payments.

Thompson went to a good friend, a creative director for a $10 million advertising agency, for advice. Should he run newspaper classifieds, print a brochure, or distribute flyers on car windshields? Of course, he had very little money to spend. Thompson heard publicity was very cost efficient. Should he try that?

Sales Letters Are Like Fishing

His friend told him that finding clients is like fishing. If you want to catch fish, you go where the fish are. If you want to clean pools, you have to go to where the pool owners are. You can reach them through their mail boxes and telephones. The advertising agency executive said the fastest and cheapest way was targeted direct mail with telemarketing follow up. In other words, Thompson needed to mail sales letters to pool owners, then call them on the telephone and say, "May I clean your pool?"

His first step was finding pool owners in the Twin Peaks area. His advertising friend showed him how to lease a reverse telephone directory from the phone company for about $150. A reverse directory lists everyone who has a phone by street address. There are no unlisted numbers in a reverse directory. Thompson then drove the streets and made a check by every address that had a pool. Now he had a list of pool owners in his neighborhood.

Next came the letter—or rather, letters. Thompson's ad pal told him why he needed to make an offer to the pool owners to generate trials. Some good offers to try would be: free consultation, first visit for only $5, and two pool cleanings for the price of one. The trick, said the advertising executive, was to turn the reader on within ninety seconds. The rest of the letter had a real WIIFM approach: "What's in it for me, the pool owner?" Not only did Thompson promise less work for the pool owner, but a safer pool because of his certification in handling chemicals. Different versions of the basic sales letter were prepared to test the different offers and to see which one attracted the most customers. A sample of this letter, and others, are included at the end of the chapter.

Thompson then mailed the letters in batches of fifty. Within three days of their receipt of the letter, he called the pool owners. Many were very happy to find someone who could handle this chore for them. Within a few days he soon had more customers than he could handle.

Trash the Phrase Junk Mail

Some would call Thompson's letters junk mail. We say let's stamp out the term junk mail posthaste. Please note that today about nine out of ten Americans are ordering through the mail. A speaker at a national direct-mail conference recently reported that the average cost of an in-person sales call is three-hundred dollars, a telephone sales call is eight dollars, and the average business-to-business direct mail piece is fifty cents. It's no wonder students in coauthor Henry's direct-mail classes report they have ordered everything from hot-air balloons to horse semen through the mail.

Junk mail is not junk; it fills needs. Thompson's newfound customers were people who wanted someone responsible to clean their pools; they just didn't have time to look. Most consumers suffer from an affliction called time famine. There is just not enough time to get it all done, especially shopping. Our ancestors were correct when they predicted that by the year 2001 we would be working half time—twelve hours a day, seven days a week. Thank goodness there are direct-mail services, 800 numbers, credit card ordering, and money-back guarantees to save us time.

There's another direct mail advantage. Each day, 1,500 newspaper, radio, and television ads bombard us and demand our clientele's attention. A direct-mail letter is ready when your potential clients are.

Here are nine secrets to make direct mail work better in the 1990s. (To paraphrase Ken Blanchard, author of *The One-Minute Manager*, they're mostly common sense, but we call them secrets because most people act as though they never knew them.)

Secret One: Our Friend the Computer

Today's biggest force in direct marketing is the computer database. Thanks to the microchip, we don't need to advertise to everybody just to reach somebody. Already 180 million Americans are in a computer database. That means whomever you want to target, you can find.

In the book *Maximarketing*, by Stan Rapp and Thomas Collins, the authors explain how public databases have already done the hard work for you. These databases have "identified by name and address just about every household worth bothering with that uses your product category but does not use your brand. Or [whoever] has exactly the hobbies or equipment or lifestyle your product or service calls for."

This all sounds well and good, but how does the novice tap into databases? If you just want to use a list, you can find one from either a directory or by using a list broker. To capitalize on the power of databases, you need to find a list compiler who uses computers to enhance mailing lists.

First let's examine the straight list route. Standard Rate and Data Service at (800) 323-8079 publishes a two-volume set that contains about fifty thousand compiled lists. Oxbridge Communications at (212) 741-0231 also has a comprehensive book of available lists. These directories offer a nearly limitless range of both consumer and business lists. Some of the categories include

> magazine subscribers
> new-home purchasers
> doctors
> automobile owners
> registered voters
> college alumni
> frequent flyers

Prices range anywhere from fifteen to three-hundred dollars per thousand names, but you can expect to pay around thirty to fifty dollars per thousand names for a typical list. How do you know the difference between a good list and a not-so-good list? This is where an independent list broker can help. It is wise to tap into these professionals' direct-mail expertise.

A second database possibility is closer to home. These are the customers you already have, which are a professional firm's most valuable asset. You have to improve your in-house use of databases to be competitive in the 1990s. If you haven't done so already, you should start a database. You can bet that your competition is doing this.

Past buyers are excellent candidates to purchase again. Current customers are outstanding referral sources. Potential buyers who have attended speeches or responded to publicity should be cultivated through direct mail. Put them on the computer. Also, prospects you have visited are excellent targets for follow-up mailings. When you collect business cards at events, put them in the database.

There is a lot of software that can help you set up your own in-house database and direct-mail efforts. These programs can show you

- How to use carrier routes for lowest cost mailing.
- The best ninety-nine dollar mailing list manager.
- How to verify addresses and add Zip + 4.
- How to instantly look up UPS and postal rates.

Secret Two: the 40-40-20 Rule

Direct-mail pioneer Ed Mayer is credited with coining the 40-40-20 rule. Simply put, 40 percent of your success will be determined by how well you define your audience. Another 40 percent will be determined by how the audience responds to how it perceives your product, service, and offer. The final 20 percent is determined by the creative package, which includes copywriting, artwork, and how it is mailed.

The Roni Hicks & Associates agency successfully used the 40-40-20 direct-mail rule to help launch and position Fairbanks Ranch as one of the nation's most prestigious communities. Stage one of the overall marketing effort was to sell custom lots at this master-planned community in Rancho Santa Fe, an exclusive enclave just north of San Diego. Since 40 percent of their success depended on targeting the right audience, a list was compiled of 1,000 of the area's wealthiest and most socially active individuals. The list was culled from those who attended local $500-per-plate charity black-tie fund-raising events.

Another 40 percent of the effort's success depended on the offer. The agency chose to test an offer of a guided tour of Fairbanks Ranch and a complimentary luncheon at the exclusive Fairbanks Ranch Country Club, site of the 1984 Olympic Equestrian Endurance Event.

The final 20 percent hinged on the creative package. A one-page letter accompanied by a four-color brochure was tested. The results: a tremendous 10 percent response rate. And thanks to targeting, every individual was prequalified. Publicity and advertising in the media communicate to everyone, even those you don't want. With direct mail you can target only those individuals you want to reach. In this case, only people who regularly pay $500 to attend charity galas.

Secret Three: You're on My List

Great direct mail requires people with a little Sherlock Holmes in them. Unfortunately, most novice businesspeople approach list research like Inspector Clouseau.

A classic story was reported by Neil Morgan in the *San Diego Tribune:* "At La Valencia Hotel, brochures were mailed to a prospective guest who wrote for information. The envelope came back from Springfield, Missouri, stamped 'cannot deliver without inmate registration number.'"

Varying direct mail lists can change response rates from plus or minus 100 to 1,000 percent.

Remember to think suspects and not prospects. Prospects are people who have expressed some interest in the product. For high-ticket items, the goal of the direct mail effort is usually to get prospects to raise their hands and say they are interested. Then a salesperson follows up.

But a suspect is different. This is a person you suspect might be a prospect. For increased response rates, put your creative efforts into the hunt for suspects. The best suspects are clones of your current customers. The more you know about them, the more clues you have to find suspects.

There are four ways to obtain lists.

1. Compile the list yourself—sometimes the only way.

2. Obtain the list from a professional compiler. (Use directories listed below or consult the Yellow Pages under "Mailing Lists.")

3. Rent someone else's list such as a magazine's subscription list or a retailer's customer list.

4. Exchange lists with others. (Museums, art galleries, and theaters do this a lot.)

To find a local list broker, look under "mailing lists" in the Yellow Pages. Talk to them about how you can tap into databases that go beyond a typical list. Here are some pros to call to get you started. American Consumer Lists of Omaha, Nebraska, has information on 82 of the nation's 91 million households, including 4.5 million high-income Americans. Call (402) 593-4640 to find out how you can take your message directly to the prospect's front door. Or Best Mailing Lists of New York City invites marketers to call (800) 692-2378 for a free consultation about the 88 million consumers and 10 million business names it has on its database.

Secret Four: Make Me an Offer

Q: What do you get when you cross the Godfather with an attorney?
A: You get an offer you can't understand.

In direct mail it's crucial to have an offer that is quickly and easily understood. Offers are really a combination of the product and service, the price and payment terms, incentives that you throw in, and any specific conditions.

To understand offers, you have to understand why people buy. Everyone has some sales experience. It was helpful to Henry that as a former salesperson he has sold everything from Fuller Brush products door to door to magazine subscriptions by phone. What motivates people to buy from a real live human being is the same as what works through the mail. Here is a tip on how to find great offers. Read books on selling. Then translate that information to your situation. Direct mail advertising is, and always has been, salesmanship in print. Think of what special proposition you would use to motivate a customer if you were face to face. Then mail that offer to many potential customers.

If your business has a sales force, talk to them. Ask them what works and what doesn't. But don't stop there. Listening to sales tip cassette programs from such sales training greats as Zig Ziglar and Tony Alessandra can also help you to formulate offers.

Secret Five: Fourteen Proven Offers

At this point you might think this all sounds so cheesy; you are marketing a sophisticated product. The principles still apply—you just need to use them in a sophisticated fashion. Only use cheesy offers if you are selling cheese. The following offers work whether you are selling pencils or penthouses, accounting or architecture.

Free Trial—Pulls two-to-one over money-back guarantee.
Free Information—Great tool to get prospects to raise their hands.
Sample—If they try it they might like it.
Conditional Sale—Send it now and bill me.
Club Offer—Like book- and record-of-the-month clubs.
Contests—Use prizes that relate.
Time Limit—You must act within thirty days.
Guaranteed Buy-Back—Return in thirty days for full refund.
Yes-No-Maybe—If maybe, send more information.
Discount—Value already must be established.
Charter—Be the first for a lifetime of value.
Piggyback—Buy now and we'll throw something extra in with the order.
Bounce Back—Upon delivery ask what else they would like to order.
Free Gift—Once you have bought, tough to get out.

We recommend direct-mail packages with the following elements: letter on nice stationery, some piece of collateral material like a brochure or reprint of a favorable news article, and a response card that does what all good salespeople do: it asks for the order.

Typically about three-by-five inches in size, this card completely explains the offer and what to do. If separated from the rest of the package, this card should be able to stand alone and sell the offer. Likewise, the letter should have all the information the prospect needs, including what to do and how to respond.

Some Free Advice on Offers

"The sun comes up and the sun goes down, and nothing else is free" goes the old adage. But that doesn't mean we stop looking.

Providing something for free works magic. Here is a list of free offers that you should test with your direct-mail efforts.

1. Free trial
2. Free gift for inquiring
3. Free information
4. Free brochure
5. Free demonstration
6. Free catalog
7. Free gift for buying
8. Free gift choice
9. Free mystery gift
10. Free fact kit
11. Free needs analysis
12. Free sample
13. Free cost estimate
14. Free sample lesson
15. Free meal
16. Free initial consultation
17. Free first issue

For information on what offers work, we recommend the direct mail chapter in *The Young & Rubicam Traveling Creative Workshop*, by Harley Norins.

Secret Six: Establish USP ASAP, OK?

Part of any great offer is your product or service's USP: unique selling proposition. This is what you offer that is different from anyone else. It's been said that if you don't have something unique to advertise about your business, advertise your business for sale.

What sets you apart from the competition? Again, ask the sales force. When they are eyeball-to-eyeball with the prospect and it's time to close the deal, what works?

Reed Trencher has a unique selling proposition for public relations services: pay-only-for-results publicity. Since 1981 Trencher's firm, Primetime Publicity and Media Consulting Corporation of Mill Valley, California, has set itself apart from the more than 1,600 traditional public relations agencies in America. Clients pay only for publicity, and only after it has been published or aired.

Most public relations agencies charge clients set monthly fees for a variety of services rendered, everything from creating brochures to staging press conferences. But Trencher's clients pay set rates for television, radio, magazine, and newspaper coverage.

Such clients as Blue Diamond, the Sharper Image, and Carnival Cruises, have used Primetime to gain feature coverage on "The Today Show," "Entertainment Tonight," and in the *Wall Street Journal*. Placements can run as high as $20,000.

On the other end of the public relations agency spectrum is Vanguard Communications, a Washington, D.C., firm specializing in what Stephan Miller, president, calls "history-making mega-events designed with a view toward changing public opinion and influencing public policy."

In April 1989 Miller staged a $1 million protest for the homeless. Its aim was to persuade Congress to restore nearly $25 billion in federal housing assistance funds cut since 1981. Gone are the days of hand-lettered placards and megaphones. Miller, an expert in creating events ideal for TV news, utilized a forty-by-sixty-foot stage complete with a rented hundred-thousand-dollar sound system.

"When Donald Trump opened up the Eastern Shuttle, he used the same methodology," Miller told the *Charlotte Observer*. "He has advance people. He has celebrity coordinators. He has caterers. The only difference is we're selling the idea that this government should pay more attention to the problem of homelessness. Donald Trump is selling airline tickets. We're selling hope."

Both Trencher and Miller operate successful firms. They have little else in common, except for the fact that each has a clearly defined unique selling proposition he can use in sales letters to potential customers.

Secret Seven: Creative Platform Diving

You don't buy coal, you buy heat.
You don't buy circus tickets, you buy thrills.
You don't buy a paper, you buy news.
You don't buy spectacles, you buy vision.
(Anonymous)

Perceptions are everything. Especially when it comes to direct mail. Your readers can't touch, taste, smell, or hear the product. They *can* read about it and see a picture. The four keys for the creative platform must be to establish the perceived

1. availability,
2. authority,
3. value, and
4. satisfaction.

Perceived availability convinces the reader that what you offer is exclusive, hard to find, or brand new. This works well for a grand opening or for the release of a new product.

Perceived authority explains why you are the best one to offer this. This is where credentials come into play. No one else should be able to make this claim.

Perceived value deals with the golden scale we all have in our minds. This is the scale that weighs benefits against cost.

Building perceived value was of critical importance for Renaissance–La Jolla, a 2,500-home master-planned community consisting solely of multifamily housing. For the groundbreaking, McKellar Development and Ahmanson Developments, Inc., mailed gift boxes to a compiled list of media, community opinion leaders, and elected officials. Inside each was an elegant mask and an invitation to a tented luncheon featuring Renaissance fare, medieval minstrels, and a commedia dell'arte troupe. A goal-exceeding 300 plus were in attendance, and the event generated positive publicity.

Perceived satisfaction means that there will be no problems. Nordstrom has built this reputation today, but Sears has been the pioneer in no-hassle returns since the Sears & Roebuck catalog days. If you have excellent customer service, sell this fact. If you have a high number of satisfied repeat buyers, let it be known.

Secret Eight: This Is Only a Test

Always test, test, test. But only test what is important, not trivial. That's the advice of Freeman Gosden, author of a tremendous book titled *Direct Marketing Success*. Gosden says there are 200 factors that affect the success or failure of any mailing.

Here is what *not* to test: color of paper stock, texture of paper, two color vs. three color, blue vs. black signature, metered mail vs. bulk rate, and one- vs. two-color reply cards. Each one of these factors is too insignificant to make a major difference in your success rates. So what should you test?

The offer and the list combined account for 80 percent of success or failure of your direct mail endeavor. Test various offers to determine a champion. Compare these against major changes in the list criteria. Now you are testing something that matters.

Secret Nine: Four Cautions

If you are serious about using direct mail to promote your business, attend a full-day seminar on the subject. One of the best is offered by Bob Hemmings, who helped found the largest direct response agency in the West. In his seminar he says there are four cautions to remember about direct mail.

The first is **there are no pat answers.** This is an art, not a science. However, we can approach this art form with scientific testing.

The second caution is **computers can't do your thinking for you.** Have you ever seen a person with a disorganized mess who decided to computerize? That person soon had a very fast disorganized mess. Computers are not capable of creative thought. That's what keeps marketing people employed.

The third point to remember is that direct mail is a **"what works" medium more than a "why it works" medium.** We can't explain why one offer works better than another. We just know through testing that it does.

A final caution is that mail is **not the only direct response medium.** These same secrets apply to print, radio, television, and telemarketing. Research shows that they work best when used together.

Getting Down to Brass Plaques, or There's Mortar to Come

One final thought. The trick is how to do this without being boring. Here's one example.

What price immortality? Well, for $100 the Gaslamp Quarter Theatre Company in San Diego was willing to let patrons see their names up in bricks.

Located in an historic turn-of-the-century section of downtown, the theatre staged an unusual fund-raising campaign when it reconstructed a new playhouse from the circa 1912 red brick San Diego Paper Box Company.

Subscribers and single performance ticket buyers made up the list. The offer was a tongue-in-cheek combination of a discount offer, a contest, a charter membership, and an invitation to a free event. This letter quickly raised $30,000 for the new building and enjoyed a 5.5 percent response. The creative approach speaks for itself. A copy of this letter is included in the samples at the end of this chapter.

TWIN PEAKS
POOL SERVICE

Dear Pool Owner,

You can have a clean pool without the work.

Keeping a pool nice is not easy. You have to worry about harsh chemicals, equipment breakdowns, and the hard-to-stop algae. But there is an easier way.

Let me do the work. And you can have the fun.

You will have a factory-certified pool technician working for you. That means you can feel safe that your heaters, filters, pumps, and other pool equipment are being handled by a pro.

You will have a cleaner, safer pool because I use only high-quality chemicals.

The kind of chemical you use does make a difference. You will save money with chemicals that don't harm your heater, filter, or pool plaster. It stops eye and skin irritation, too.

You also feel good knowing your pool is in the hands of a dependable, local pool pro.

You can count on me to be on time each week. And if you need special help fast, I can be there right away.

You will see the difference. That's why I want to make you this special offer:

FIRST FULL-SERVICE VISIT FOR $5

Try me for only $5, with no obligation. Your pool will be vacuumed, the tile scrubbed, the walls brushed, the equipment inspected, and the water chemistry tested with our thorough five-step evaluation.

Please call me at 748-7245 to set a good time to see you.

Sincerely,

Martin Thompson

Owner

P.S. Your "first full-service visit for only $5" offer expires August 15. Please call me to arrange an appointment at 748-7245 today. (If your pool isn't finished being built, hang on to this ad, we'll honor it when you're ready.)

GASLAMP
QUARTER
THEATRE
COMPANY

Dear Friend and Theatre Lover:

The whole idea for this party invitation hit us like a ton of bricks. Well, more like 300 bricks.

Would you like to . . .

Win a free stay at an historic Victorian hotel?

Attend a slightly naughty 1880s-style soirée?

Enjoy an unheard-of dinner special at a great new restaurant?

And become immortal by having your name up in bricks?

This could happen to you if you purchase a brick at our new Deane Theatre. Think of the immortality you'll gain with your name on a brick! And picture the incomparable thrill of pointing to your brick and exclaiming, "That's my brick!" You'll want to take a picture of it to impress your friends and enrage your enemies.

You see, we recently sold bricks to raise funds for the new Deane Theatre, being built next to the Horton Grand Hotel. These are no ordinary bricks; they are *historic* bricks dating back to 1912. More than that, each brick bears the name of the lucky person who bought it and who will be part of our new theatre.

The brick sale was a big success, but there's no pleasing some people.

In spite of having sold about half of these remarkable bricks, we got the message from Ernie Hahn, the downtown developer, and Charles Deane, for whom the theatre is named. Together they have raised almost $1 million for the theatre. They suggested that more people be given an opportunity to buy these commemorative gems of masonry. *Actually, what they said was, "Sell more bricks!"*

An Incredible Offer!

We're halfway to our goal of selling the 300 bricks. Think of it! A chance to have your very own brick with a brass plaque inscribed with your name. The brick will be part of the new Deane Theatre, for all to see and envy.

You won't find these bricks in stores. They're available *only* in this extraordinary, once-in-a-lifetime offer.

Prices Slashed!

You'd expect to pay a lot more for these amazing bricks that once were part of the old Paper Box Company.

They're packed with history! They were around when Ida Bailey was queen of the (in)famous Stingaree. They stayed dry during Prohibition. They stood up under the 1929 crash. They remained stone-faced during FDR's New Deal. They watched the opening of our first Gaslamp Quarter Theatre, the rise of Horton Plaza, and the rebuilding of the Horton Grand Hotel. Now they are being used to rebuild our new theatre.

You'd guess these brick treasures would easily be worth $300 or more. But you won't have to pay $300. You won't have to pay $200. You won't even have to pay the regular price of $100. Because now, during this limited time offer, you can have the brick of your choice for only $99.43!

FREE! A PICK-A-BRICK PARTY!

You're invited to join us for a fantastic party from 4 to 7 p.m., August 19. Place: The courtyard of the Horton Grand Hotel, at Fourth and Island. This beautifully restored Victorian hotel reigned regally in the 1880s and does so once again.

This letter is your FREE ADMISSION to the party that will feature complimentary 1880-era hors d'oeuvres and a no-host bar.

During the party you can pick up the brick(s) you want. Or just come to the party and judge the bricks.

There's no obligation to buy any of the bricks on display.

Wait! There's More!

There is a valuable bonus for you if you order now at our rock-bottom—brick-bottom—prices. Buy *two* bricks at our sensationally reduced price of just $99.43 each, and you'll get a *third* brick for only *$49.99*. How's that for a break on bricks? Prices will never be lower. So act now!

Stage Door Alley, Your Brick's New Home

What is Stage Door Alley? It's a colorful walkway between the new Deane Theatre and the Horton Grand Hotel. At night, this fascinating alcove will be illuminated by festive lanterns, spreading warm light across show posters, banners, and Victorian artwork. During intermissions at the Deane Theatre, Stage Door Alley will offer bar service and concessions. Playgoers will also be able to view the names of theatre donors inscribed on the 1912 bricks.

WIN A ROOM WITH A VIEW (of your brick)

When you buy a brick for our fund-raising program, your name will *automatically* be entered in a contest to win a FREE overnight stay at the magnificent Horton Grand Hotel.

And yes, your room will have a splendid view of your own brick. The prize includes *ten tickets* to a theatre performance for the night of the free stay. This means you could invite a group of guests to see a show and your brick on the same night!

You are also eligible for the contest even if you do not buy a brick. Just register the night of the party. There is no obligation. Prizes will be awarded in a drawing to be held at 6 p.m. on Tuesday, August 19. You need not be present to win.

But That's Not All!

When you buy a brick during our closeout sale, you'll get a special premium: a *$10 dinner gift certificate* for the IDA BAILEY RESTAURANT in the Horton Grand Hotel.

The menu is right out of the Nineteenth Century, with traditional favorites including Yankee Pot Roast, Chicken and Dumplings, and Apple Brown Betty, with dinners starting at $9.95, and the libations served 1880s style.

This gastronomic house of pleasure is situated on the site of another well-known "house"—that of Ida Bailey, infamous madam. But Ida was not the only famed personage seen on this site. Sip your favorite libation at the Palace Bar and you'll get another taste of history. Because legendary figures like Babe Ruth, George Raft, Joe Louis, and Jack Dempsey all hung out here.

Meet Ida and Her Girls

The courtyard party on August 19 will be livened up with a personal appearance by "Ida Bailey" (remarkably well preserved for a woman over 100) and her girls. When you see this beautiful entourage, you'll realize that the good old days looked pretty good after all.

What Satisfied Brick-Buyers Say . . .

Still undecided about buying a brick for the new Deane Theatre? Just look at these unsolicited testimonials.

"I always wanted a brick when I was a child. Now that I have one, I realize how much I had missed."
Roni Hicks

"My brick has changed my life. Sometimes I wish I could bring my brick to the City Council."
Abbe Wolfsheimer

"Bricks are super gift ideas. They're great stocking stuffers at Christmas."
Morley Golden

"I visit my brick as often as I can. It always seems glad to see me."
Tom Blair

Limited Quantity. Move Fast!

With half of the 300 Deane Theatre bricks already sold, time is running out! When the short supply is gone, that's it. No more will ever be available. And we know you'll never forgive yourself if you miss out on this tremendous opportunity.

Four Ways to Buy

To make sure your brick(s) will be reserved for you, please order today. Just fill in the order card and mail it in the enclosed, postpaid envelope.

There are four easy ways to buy Deane Theatre bricks. Use your VISA or MasterCard. Enclose your check, or use our special 25 plan ($25 down and $25 a month for three months for each brick.)

The more bricks you buy, the faster you'll move into a higher brick bracket. Remember, all purchases are tax-deductible donations.

Imagine! Your name in bricks. Can't you just see it?

Yours truly,

Kit Goldman
Managing Producer
GASLAMP QUARTER THEATRE

P.S. Because of the anticipated heavy demand, all bricks will be sold on a first-come, first-served basis. Sorry, no dealers or brokers.

Top Self-Marketing Secrets

Nine Secrets for Guaranteed Better Sales Letters

1. Learn how to access computer databases. You can find whomever you want to target with a computer.

2. Remember the 40-40-20 rule. Simply put, 40 percent of your success is the list, 40 percent is your offer, and 20 percent is your creative approach.

3. For greater success, put your creative energies into the hunt for lists of good potential customers.

4. In direct mail, the offer is crucial. Good offers are a combination of the product or service, the price and payment terms, incentives that you throw in, and any specific conditions.

5. Use the list of fourteen proven offers to brainstorm ones that will work for you.

6. Discover your unique selling proposition. Determine what sets you apart from the competition and highlight it.

7. Perceptions are everything. Establish in the mind of the reader perceived availability, authority, value, and satisfaction.

8. Test only what is important, not what is trivial. Test the offer and the lists, which account for 80 percent of success or failure.

9. Four cautions: there are no pat answers; computers can't do your thinking; remember what works and forget why it works; and mail is not the only direct response medium.

12

If at First You Don't Succeed, Try a Gimmick
Some Offbeat Marketing Ploys

When Tom Churm, a twenty-something advertising copywriter in New York City, last went looking for work, he sent a message that couldn't be ignored. Potential Madison Avenue employers received a can of Alpo with a note pasted on the label: "Please give me a job so I don't have to keep eating this."

Actually Churm's gimmick wasn't too far from the truth. *Adweek* magazine reported that his home was a welfare hotel on Manhattan's Upper West Side and his diet consisted primarily of generic macaroni-and-cheese dinners, which is not too far up the food chain from dog chow. Churm's attention-grabber worked, and the University of Colorado at Boulder grad now creates ads for such clients as Planned Parenthood and Everlast. Although Churm still lives at the same welfare hotel, his menu choices have greatly improved.

All this is offered as food for thought about self-marketing through gimmicks. These ploys work when you need to capture someone's attention. Once you have that attention, it is up to you to deliver. Style alone will not put groceries on your table in this dog-eat-dog food world if you don't have the goods to back it up. But first you must be heard by the decision makers. As ad great David Oglivy says, "You can't save souls in an empty church." Or as we say, "Without a little style who will know if you have any substance?"

Here is another example to whet your appetite. In the early 1980s, Reaganomics gave Michael Sands, owner of a gourmet bakery called C'est Cheesecake in Los Angeles, an idea for a promotional gimmick. "I called up all the media and said I was going to give away cheesecake for fifty cents to counter the Reagan depression," Sands told *Entrepreneur* magazine. "I had 1,500 people lined up to buy my cheesecake, and the television crew and press showed up. It was a great promotion."

Sands, a former fashion model and actor, isn't above a little personal cheesecake to promote his products. Getting the attention of retailers for new food products is a tough job. When he came out with a new cookie, Sands exposed himself to the cameras to create a nude poster of himself holding a strategically placed sign that introduced "The First Gourmet White Chocolate Chip Cookie." The result was new outlets and a *People* magazine feature on Sands in its food section.

Sands admits that promotion will only take you so far. You must have a good product to promote, which is why he always sends along a sample. "You always have to send your product along with your proposal," says Sands. "If you are a shoe manufacturer, you send a shoe. I do that not only to get the coverage by the media, but also to get into retail outlets." It was this strategy that landed Sands' creations in big West Coast grocery chains, like Ralphs and Vons, and then 7-Eleven convenience stores.

Other Sands gimmicks have included giving away bags of white chocolate chip cookies on "National Chocolate Chip Cookie Day," using a boy dressed as a mouse to deliver gourmet cheesecake to actress Shelley Winters, packaging small cheesecakes with designer labels and calling them "Baby Cakes," and conducting a national search for a Baby Cakes poster girl ("the Charlie girl of cheesecakes"). All received excellent media coverage, with a little help from Sands.

"When you can't afford an ad campaign, all this other stuff is available," says Sands. "Everyone knows somebody who can help him in this area, whether it's in the conception of an idea or getting the media interested. People on newspaper, television, and radio station staffs are willing to help you. Use all of these people. Don't be afraid to ask."

If You Don't Ask, You Don't Get

Great salespeople always seem to credit their success to two main actions: consistently prospecting and then consistently asking for the order. Prospecting is the activity that gets your concept before the right people. In self-marketing, that can be potential customers, clients, retailers, distributors, and the media. And every time you get in front of a prospect, you need to ask for the order. This means saying in no uncertain terms what you would like him or her to do for you.

Sometimes what you will want is information. Just ask. People will usually tell you anything you want to know if you just ask. People are flattered to be the center of attention, and your questions give them an opportunity to shine. Sales trainer Tony Alessandra says, if you don't ask, you don't get. Use gimmicks to get the attention of the right people, then nicely ask for what you want.

Another key concept is to find ways to keep asking. A former newspaper reporter, coauthor Henry was taught to find different ways to ask for what he wanted. It works with information and works with new business development and other delights in life.

To illustrate the point, he tells the story about one of his prized possessions. If you have ever priced custom neon signs, you know they are expensive. Henry wanted a neon sign with his name on it and found such an item at a restaurant, advertising Henry Weinhardt's Private Reserve, a regional beer from Portland, Oregon. The restaurant manager declined to sell it and told Henry that it was brewery policy not to sell signs, either.

But Henry's motto is keep asking, so he called to ask the brewery, and the receptionist said no. So he asked who ordered the signs for the brewery and was transferred to merchandising. They also said no. "By the way," he asked, "who do you order the signs from?" The merchandising rep told him the name of the firm; the phone number; the contact's name, Ken; and her name, Maria.

"Hello, Ken," Henry began the call, "I just talked to Maria up in merchandising at the brewery and I need to order one of those Henry's signs." The neon sign, purchased at the brewery's volume discount price, was soon hand-delivered to Henry in San

Diego. If you really want it, then it pays to keep asking, as the next example illustrates.

When in Doubt, Send Money

Ron Seaver was a restaurant manager with one goal in life: to work for the San Diego Padres baseball team. Getting a job in baseball is like being discovered in Hollywood. Too many hopefuls chasing too few jobs.

Hearing that the best chance to get in was through ticket sales, Seaver sent his résumé to the appropriate team executive. His application stacked up with the many others received that day and every other day of the year. Seaver received the standard rejection letter. He decided to try the creative approach.

Seaver attached a check for $50 to the rejection letter and sent it back to the executive with this note: "I'd pay anything to work for the San Diego Padres. May I have an appointment to talk about it?"

Seaver got the appointment, his check back, and a trial job in the ticket office. From there he progressed to a full-time ticket sales position with the team. Later he became director of promotions for the Padres, working with giveaway item sponsors to lure more fans to the ballpark.

Money also is used on more of a mass marketing scale to reach doctors. Finding out what your customers want is a smart business move. But what if your customers are doctors? Asking busy doctors, who can make as much as $1,000 per hour, to take time to fill out a survey you mailed them just doesn't work. Unless you try a gimmick.

Some survey companies are attaching two-dollar bills to each survey they mail to doctors. It's human nature to pocket the two-dollar bill. And if the questionnaire is not too long, the doctors evidently feel obligated to complete the survey and return it in its postage-paid return envelope.

This concept works with even less money. An executive fitness firm asked San Diego's top 150 presidents and CEOs to complete a survey in return for a quarter. Here's how it worked.

Renaissance Executive Fitness charges fifty dollars an hour to help companies get their valuable yet unhealthy executives in shape. Personal fitness trainers work individually with the flabby execs three times a week to get them on the road to fitness. Being exclusive is an important part of the Renaissance marketing strategy, and it shuns advertising in favor of publicity.

To generate publicity, a six-question survey was devised that would take busy presidents less than half a minute to complete. The objectives were to get their opinions on whether having healthy employees improved productivity and lowered absenteeism and to find out if their companies sponsored fitness programs.

Boosting awareness of Renaissance Executive Fitness with the presidents and chief executive officers of San Diego's 150 largest companies was a side benefit of the survey. Making a good impression was critical, so a newly minted quarter was glued to the following letter.

```
Would you please
take 25 seconds to
send us this survey?

Dear Chief Executive:

    Your opinion is very important to us.  We are
seeking the opinions of San Diego's presidents and
CEOs about health and fitness in the workplace.

    The survey will take 25 seconds to complete. Why
is a quarter attached to this letter? If you were
paid 1 cent for every second of the year, your annual
salary would be $315,360.  We hope this is fair
compensation.

    Please  return  the  survey  in  the  enclosed
postage-paid envelope. Thank you for your help.

Sincerely,

Nick Holslag
President
```

A surprisingly high 67 percent of the top execs completed the survey. The results made excellent material for a piece of publicity-generating research called "The Renaissance Executive Fitness Report." About 75 percent reported that fitness improved performance, but only 25 percent funded any such programs. "San Diego CEOs favor fitness but are unwilling to fund it" read the headlines in the local newspapers and business journals. The report, filled with analysis from the Renaissance president, also resulted in a local television feature and a large feature story in the top fitness trade journal. Speaking invitations soon followed.

Using quarters also paid off for the Vagabond Inns motel chain. Getting the attention of travel agents and the media was always a challenge for Vagabond. In honor of their silver twenty-fifth anniversary, the chain sent out letters with pure silver quarters from their founding year of 1958. Purchased at a coin dealer for less than a dollar apiece, these reminders of the days when Ike was President and Elvis was King were cost-effective attention grabbers.

Postcards from the Edge

Some of the most creative approaches to finding a job come from advertising copywriters. It's little wonder, since their line of work demands coming up with new twists on familiar ideas.

A copywriter decided to leave New York behind and drive to San Francisco to find work. He compiled a list of potential employers and along the way would drop each of them a postcard. He did it from places such as Cool, California, and Yale, Washington. Not only did he find a job, he later turned his postcard odyssey into a successful campaign to promote the Beef Council.

Another copywriter tried another postcard approach to a West Coast job, but he never left Toledo, Ohio. Instead he combed the thrift shops and antique stores for seventy-five-year-old unused postcards of yesteryear Toledo. These full-color illustrations of a bygone era made this job searcher stand out.

When a third copywriter decided to make the move from Las Vegas to Southern California, he went beyond the postcard. All the way to the milk carton. He produced a completely realistic half-gallon milk carton. On the side was the headline, "Have you seen this man?" His name, photo, and vital statistics were listed along with a phone number to call if one would like to see him. It quickly got him the appointments he desired. After seeing what he could do, he got a job with a successful Orange County firm.

Always a Timely Gimmick

Time also opened the door for a West Coast trust division of an aggressive bank. The trust division, which specialized in managing self-directed investment portfolios for physicians, had tried unsuccessfully for years to make a presentation to a large specialty medical group. But a timely gimmick changed that.

Research revealed that a committee of about a dozen doctors made the investment decisions for the group. An old fashioned chrome stopwatch, valued at about seventy-five dollars, was gift wrapped for each doctor. A former policeman turned private detective was hired to obtain the home addresses of the doctors, which he did with ease at a charge of less than a hundred dollars.

Each gift was sent to the doctor's home, where it wouldn't get screened by an office manager. With the gift came a note from the trust division president asking for the appointment. Stating that he understood how valuable the doctor's time was, his presentation would take less than five minutes. "Please time me with the stopwatch," he asked. The president's note explained he would only stay longer if invited by the investment committee to say more. After years of trying the conventional route, the gimmick paid off and he was granted the appointment.

When Is a Résumé Not a Résumé?

New twists on familiar ideas make the best gimmicks. Take the résumé, for instance. Many books have been written on how to write a good résumé. Other books will tell you that a résumé won't get you a job. It's just a necessary step.

Kimberly Kasitz wanted a job in public relations and used an innovative résumé to get it. As a recent college grad, her lack of experience would put her at a disadvantage when compared to other candidates. Kasitz decided the standard résumé was not the way to go.

Writing news releases is the main task of someone newly hired in the field of public relations. So to prove that she could do it, and to position herself apart from the pack, Kasitz produced a résumé in the form of a news release. The approach earned her interviews all over town. Not only did she get an immediate job, the résumé helped her build an industry network that has helped with steps up the career ladder. A copy of her news release is included at the end of this chapter.

A Grab Bag of Gimmicks

Do you have a favorite gimmick story that you would like to share? Maybe this chapter will inspire you to try something out of the ordinary. If so, please send your gimmick story to Henry and Diane at the address listed in this book. To help you be more creative, here is a grab bag of gimmick ideas.

1. When graphic artist Jeri Deneen went on vacation one year, she sent a deflated beachball to existing and potential clients with a note reading, "I'm off to the seashore for two weeks, but when I return I'll be ready to get the ball rolling again to meet your needs." The free giveaway not only kept her clients informed, but showed off her talent to those who had not yet engaged her services.

2. A sales rep from a small print shop showed her gratitude to a client who passed a big job her way by bringing in note sheets in personalized, smoked Plexiglass holders for each member of the client's staff. She dropped off the gifts early one morning without fanfare so that they would be waiting when employees arrived. The gifts were inexpensive for the printer but carried a lot of weight with the client. Everyone likes his or her business to be appreciated, but few people remember to express gratitude.

3. When a computer salesperson learned that her customer was dissatisfied with an improper installation of new equipment, she made a visit to personally learn about the problem. She brought along the repair technician and a box of ice cream bars for the

annoyed staff. The goodwill gesture helped to thaw relations—as did the fact that the salesperson didn't leave until the installation was correct.

4. The holidays are a time when everyone gives gifts, so it's important to make yours stand out from the crowd. One holiday season, Diane's company, the Gage Group, sent tire gauges to its clients with a tag reading, "Have an engaging holiday season and start the New Year on a roll." The turn-of-phrase captured lots of praise from clients who noted the agency's ingenuity—reinforcing that they were the creative team of choice.

5. If you want your message to stand out among the heap of junk mail, try an unorthodox format. When the principal of another agency merged her company with Diane's, the agency sent out a colorful Chinese take-out box with a fortune cookie inside. The outside note read, "It's our great fortune to announce that Betsy Eisele of Public Relations Prescriptions has joined the Gage Group." The fortune inside offered this note: "Sweet success and fortune are yours with public relations, marketing, and advertising from the Gage Group." The Gage Group's phone number was included.

6. Henry even believes in using unorthodox birth announcements to promote the business. He prepared a blueprint to announce the arrival of his nephew, Jace Swank. It also helped promote Henry's brother-in-law's company, Hearn and Swank Construction. Clients, referral sources, and subcontractors were reminded of the firm when they received the blueprints of this latest completed project. But even more successful was Henry's announcement for the arrival of his own first child. His parody of a horse racing program (Henry's family has been in horse racing for five generations) received coverage in the *Los Angeles Times* and *Sports Illustrated* magazine. Here is what *Sports Illustrated* reported. (The following is reprinted courtesy of *Sports Illustrated* from the September 19, 1983, issue. Copyright © 1983, Time, Inc. All rights reserved. Scorecard by Alexander Wolff.)

She Missed the Call

To herald the birth of their daughter Karla Lee, Henry DeVries, a San Diego public relations man, and his wife, Vikki, sent out announcements with a horse racing theme. Karla was identified as the entry of "DeVries Stables," the "post time" was given as 12:51 A.M. on August 10, and Mom and Dad were referred to as jockey and trainer, respectively. All very cute, but also rather puzzling to a friend of Karla's paternal grandmother. After receiving the announcement, she called to express surprise that Henry and Vikki had bought a racehorse.

FOR IMMEDIATE RELEASE

Contact: Kimberly A. Kasitz   September 19, 1985
1483 Eastside Road
El Cajon, CA 92020
(619) 448-8117

AMBITIOUS GRAD SETS SIGHTS ON RONI HICKS & ASSOCIATES

SAN DIEGO, CA—Kimberly Kasitz, a recent graduate of the University of California at San Diego, has announced plans to seek employment with Roni Hicks & Associates. Referred to the prestigious San Diego Agency by Mr. Jim Benedict, Ms. Kasitz is interested in acquiring an entry-level position in the field of public relations.

At a time when MBA graduates are being criticized for their narrow visions and lack of creativity, a broad liberal arts educations, supported by a B.A. in Political Science, has provided Ms. Kasitz with the basic analytical/problem-solving skills required to succeed in today's business world.

With a minor in writing, extensive editing experience, and a courteous yet tactful manner in dealing with the public, she has demonstrated excellent written and oral communication skills. In addition, she is highly motivated and has developed outstanding organizational/efficiency skills through her administrative work experience and participation in student organizations.

While lacking "hands on" experience in the competitive public relations industry, she is prepared to support her contentions with numerous references, letters of recommendation, and an impressive portfolio of written work. As Ms. Kasitz remarked, she strongly believes that she can fulfill the high standards required by an agency such as Roni Hicks & Associates.

#

Top Self-Marketing Secrets

Four Ways to Make Gimmicks Work

1. Ploys can only capture attention. Once you have that attention, it's up to you to deliver.

2. Once you have someone's attention, ask for the order. Say in no uncertain terms what you want him or her to do for you.

3. Don't rule out money as a gimmick. When people receive money, they feel obligated to help.

4. Clever communications to introduce yourself will go a long way. Not only do they make your name known immediately, prospects will remember you in years to come.

13

Guerrilla Advertising Tricks and Tactics
How to Outsmart Them When You Can't Outspend Them

Guerrilla advertising, like guerrilla warfare, is the strategy to use when you are hopelessly outnumbered. And when it comes to advertising dollars, all professional service businesses are outnumbered.

Guerrilla warfare is fighting by other than ordinary means in areas occupied by the enemy. Large-scale guerrilla tactics, invented by such American Revolutionary War leaders as Francis Marion, the "Swamp Fox" of South Carolina, were used to harass the British. Spanish for little war, the term "guerrilla" was coined during the Peninsular War of 1808-1814 when Napoleon could not conquer the Spanish partisans. The underground, or resistance, of World War II was actually a well-organized guerrilla campaign credited with playing a major role in the defeat of the Nazi occupation of Europe.

Guerrilla advertising means not playing by the rules of traditional advertising. The saturation advertising practiced by the McDonalds, IBMs, Coca-Colas, and Budweisers of the world is what we mean by traditional advertising. They have the big ad budgets that allow them to repeat their messages over and over and over again.

Consider all of the advertisements that you read, see, and hear in one day. From the time your clock radio wakes you up in the morning until you fall asleep watching the late news on television at night, the average American is bombarded with more than 1,500 ad messages. For the professional service that wishes to advertise, the enemy is not your competition, but the sheer volume of advertising that exists.

The two previous chapters have discussed how to make your name known through publicity. While free publicity doesn't exist—you either pay a consultant, an employee, or take time yourself to get the placements—in most instances, publicity is less expensive than paid advertising.

However, advertising does offer some advantages over publicity. With advertising you control the message and the timing. You can decide exactly what the ad will communicate and when it will be in front of prospective clients. So what is the self-marketer to do?

The Guerrilla Attitude

The first step is to accept your fate. So what if your private practice doesn't have the firepower of General Electric or General Foods? Saturation advertising isn't the answer. Because you know your niche, you can use a sharpshooter approach.

A magazine ad promoting Westwood One Companies, an umbrella group of three radio networks, says it all for us. The photo is the rear-view of a red overall-clad three-year-old boy standing over a bathroom toilet. The headline reads: "The success of target advertising, like so many things in life, is ultimately a matter of aim."

Remember, you control where the ads appear. Zealously seek out those media that carry the highest concentrations of your target audience. For the most part, mass media like television, radio, and daily newspapers will not be the way to go because you pay too much to reach people who don't matter.

If you have a service for which Yellow Pages and classified ads are appropriate, this is where the bulk of your advertising dollars should go. Everybody watches television, reads magazines, and listens to the radio. But the only people who read Yellow Pages and classifieds are those people who want to buy now.

You must make these ads convey that you are the best. This is where you should invest in the biggest size you can afford. Many prospects will make their sole judgment about how good you are by the size of your ad. For lots of good information on this subject, we recommend Jay Conrad Levinson's book, *Guerrilla Marketing: Secrets for Making Big Profits from Your Small Business.*

Levinson is a former creative director with one of the world's largest and oldest advertising agencies, J. Walter Thompson. Which brings us to another guerrilla tactic. Who says you can't afford the same talent as the big guns? In every city there are talented freelance advertising copywriters and graphic artists who once worked for big agencies. Here's how to find these people. Look up advertising agencies in the Yellow Pages. Call up a couple and ask to speak to the creative director. Tell him or her that you are looking for the names of the best freelance writers and artists in town.

By all means invest in professionals who can do the job right. Advertising, like surgery, is best left to professionals. Whatever the space or time costs, you are spending too much to try to scrimp on the creative product. And with this guerrilla tactic, you can work with superior talent for a fraction of what an agency would charge you for essentially the same caliber of work.

Covering all of the Basics: The Guerrilla Checklist

Here are some advertising basics you can use when directing and to evaluate a freelance copywriter who is working for you. We credit Steve McNamara, an advertising consultant, for the insights he imparted in "3 Ways to Influence Behavior with Print Advertisements," *Small Business Reports,* May 1989; *How to Be Your Own Advertising Agency* by Bert Holtje, McGraw Hill, 1981; and Franklin & Associates, an advertising and public relations firm. Most of these pointers work for all forms of advertising; the graphics tips are, of course, for print ads.

1. **Know your objective.**
   - Be clear about what you want to say.
   - Choose one reason for the ad.
     - Introduce a new product/service or a new feature of an existing one.

- Explain unique characteristics or the performance of a product.
- Show how a product/service is used for best results.
- Build brand loyalty or company image.
- Announce price changes, guarantees, discounts, etc.
- Maintain a good image in the heat of a crisis, e.g., recalls, shortages.

2. Be credible.
- Don't overpromise.
- Don't tell lies.
- Live up to your word.
- Use testimonials that relate a benefit to your reader; avoid bragging.
- Deliver, deliver, deliver.

3. Decide on a theme for your ad.
- Use your objective to create a theme that will pull all of your advertising points together.

4. Create a strong headline.
- Use a benefit headline such as the following:
  - "The last battery your car will ever need." (J.C. Penney)
  - "When you're out of town and out of cash, we'll be there for you." (Diner's Club)
- Make an outrageous statement. "It's hard to remain philosophical when you're number three." (Savin Corporation)
- Play on words, as a bank ad did using a photo of Prince Charles: "Taking over the family business shouldn't be a royal pain."
- Avoid negative headlines, sell positive benefits.
- Allow long headlines; research shows they sell better than shorter ones.

5. Write a lead sentence that leaves readers begging for more.
- Refer to a problem that troubles your target audience.
- Illuminate benefits—easier, richer, younger looking, saves time, sets you apart.

- Get them involved in a story.
- Use statistics for an "ah ha!" reaction.
- Tickle their funny bone. (In a *USA Today* survey, a Federal Express ad had good results when it told of a FedEx employee who could track a package around the world but couldn't find his glasses. Toyota got rave reviews for an ad based on the idea of West German carmakers spying on a Toyota Celica.)

6. Use a tone appropriate for your audience.
- Speak directly to the audience, use the word "you."
- Employ some of the dozen magic words:

save	results	health	proven
new	discover	money	you
love	free	easy	guarantee

- Use language appropriate for your audience.

7. Write explicit body copy.
- Describe the color, size, fashionability of a product, or the need for and advantages of a service.
- Don't sell features, sell benefits. As someone once said, "Sell the sizzle—not the steak."
- Press one of the dozen "hot buttons" that get customers to buy.

sex	privacy	family	recreation
ego	prestige	finances	security
love	convenience	investment	culture

- Be specific; facts sell.
- List your price; readers overestimate prices not listed. Emphasize savings, and describe payment options.

8. Develop an attractive layout.
- A smaller ad with a colored headline can dominate a black-and-white page.
- A bold headline or photo set in the center and surrounded by white space captures attention.
- Create a strong, dominant focal point that can grab attention and pull people into the ad.

- Use illustrations to draw reader attention—photos increase recall about 25 percent over artwork.
- Make a point with before-and-after photos that show either a change in a person or performance due to a superior product.
- Include a strong logo, company name, address, and phone number.
- Let there be white space to give your reader room to breathe.

9. **Ask for the order. If you don't ask, you don't get.**
   - Tell your would-be customers what to do, where to go, and what number to call. (Toll-free is best.)
   - Include a coupon for direct response.

10. **Conduct a pretest to gauge customer response; then alter accordingly.**

11. **Track results.**
    - Know where your business is coming from. Did the ad pull?
    - Use lures like, "Bring this ad in for...." or lines like, "Mention you heard this ad and save...."
    - Remember an increase in sales takes time. Repeat the message. To measure effectiveness, use different strategies and compare results.

When you've come up with an ad concept you like, ask yourself these questions posed by *Small Business Reports.*

1. Are the benefits of buying clearly spelled out and is the message persuasive?

2. Is the ad properly directed to the target market?

3. Is the campaign consistent with the image you want to convey?

After your ad has run, critique it by answering these questions.

1. Is there any measurable evidence that the ad is, or is not, working?

2. What would have been the likely sales level without the campaign?

3. Did the campaign meet all sales objectives?

Let's Make a Deal

Just as in direct mail, the offer is one of the most important parts of advertising. Sometimes an outrageous offer is necessary to gain the foot traffic you need. Take a lead from millionaire Bob Stupak. Owner of Vegas World's two new towers, Stupak extended the "comp" concept of giving big gamblers complimentary rooms, drinks, and shows to the average family, making a luxurious vacation within their reach.

If you can believe Stupak's advertorial, more than one-half million people have taken advantage of the offer that includes a $1,000 casino action bankroll. "A few high rollers will gamble enough to cover the cost of your entire vacation," Stupak says of his business gamble. "It always happens this way, always will."

What can you give away to get people into your place of business? Department stores call this a loss leader. Can you offer a free telephone consultation? A free thirty-day trial? Free delivery? A special report? A discount on a class?

Tell Me a Story

They look like articles. They read like articles. But the space they take up isn't free like articles. They're advertorials—that hybrid of advertisement and editorial that cries "Gotcha! We tricked you into reading this!" when the reader at last spots the fine print "advertisement" on the page.

But advertorials work because they pull readers in through the age-old art of storytelling. Anecdotes, quotes, feelings, and thoughts are powerful tools to get consumers to make buying decisions—kind of like a third-party endorsement.

Most essential in an advertorial is that you have an interesting story, according to Richard Ensman's article, "Tales from Your Business: A New Approach to Advertising," in the August 1985, *Entrepreneur.* That means it "touches the reader in some way. It gets him excited, interested, happy, or hopeful. It moves him—to joy or sorrow, to challenge or to immediate action."

Be sure that the writing in your advertorial is succinct, like a good magazine article. And just like magazine writing, the lead paragraph has to be a hook that grabs and, for a moment, makes the reader forget everything else but your story. Then write intriguing prose that includes descriptive adjectives and active verbs. Ensman says, "Dramatize your product, but be realistic. Well-written descriptions of your product create desire on the part of the reader. And when you begin to show how your product can help with your potential customer's image, efficiency, or standing, your sale is half made."

Major players in the advertising game are using a new form of storytelling that involves getting customers to write the stories themselves. "Maalox moments," created by the antacid of the same name, asked consumers to write in with their searing stress tales. The ad agency turns the best letters—some of which have been three pages, single spaced—into ads with actors playing out the scene. Since the ad began in the summer of 1989, Maalox claimed the number one spot in market share at 15 percent. (*USA Today*, April 3, 1990).

Levi Strauss & Company, did the same thing when it asked consumers aged twelve to twenty-four to write or call to answer the question, "What are you doing in our jeans?" Winners will be paid to appear in the ads showing real kids being themselves in the Levi products, according to Daniel Chew, Levi's marketing manager.

Again *USA Today* reports that marketers hope that, by involving consumers in the creative process, the ads become more involving. These stories of real people give ads an extra dose of truth. (*USA Today*, Wednesday, May 23, 1990).

One of the best examples of storytelling that isn't in advertorial form but is designed like an ad, yet with a headline and byline, is for Vaseline Pure Petroleum Jelly. Chesebrough-Ponds, Inc., created this ad that has all the touches—the intriguing lead, descriptive adjectives, and active verbs.

The Hollywood Skin Drench

By Lisa Nixon

I was staying with an old school friend who married a famous film producer. After flying five hours, my skin seemed very dry. Amanda took one look at my rough, flaky arms, then bolted upstairs. She came back with an old sweat suit and a jar of Vaseline Petroleum Jelly. "Here, go take a shower and smooth this all over your body. Put on the sweat suit and read for a while." And so I did. Amanda said that when she told her dermatologist about this treatment, he explained that without a prescription, even he couldn't recommend anything better for overdry skin. When I took off the sweat suit, I was amazed. My skin had a new smoothness, a softness that reminded me of my teenage years. Later, I asked Amanda which movie star told her about the Hollywood Skin Drench. "Darling," she chuckled, "in Bel Air, we never name names."

We have proof that the ad works. Reading this story as she wrote this chapter inspired Diane to slather Vaseline on her dry, aching feet and cover them in big thick socks. Is Chesebrough-Ponds looking for more testimonials?

ADC Stoorza, a Southern California ad agency, used a different form of storytelling in promoting Carlos Murphy restaurants. The account team used pictures of exciting places like the "Land of Burrito Towers" and "Frijole Wells" on postcards with a handwritten message. One of these ads read:

Hey Guys:

You wouldn't believe this place. You can walk out on the rocks right up to the falls, hold out

a tortilla chip and just like that you've got
guacamole and chips! It tastes great, unless you
got some with a tree limb floating in it. Too bad
there isn't a Margarita stream running alongside.
Your vagabond correspondent, Carlos.

Badvertising: It Wastes Bucks Every Time

Just as important as the do's of advertising are the don'ts—those
"badvertising" pitfalls that we all must avoid if we want to stretch,
not waste, ad dollars.

Don't make your customers work to get in touch with you. Just
before the Christmas holidays, a portrait company with multiple
shopping mall outlets sent out a generic advertising promotion to
homeowners with small children in a number of cities. Each piece
had the name of the shopping mall closest to the recipient's home
stamped on it, but no phone number could be found. In the few
days one mother put off looking up the phone number in the
Yellow Pages, a school portrait flyer came to the house. Since all
she had to do was pop money in an envelope for her child to take
to school, she chose that portrait route—even though she knew that
the other photo would offer more choices and a better quality.

An entertainment coupon book failed similarly. In a four-color
magazine ad touting its virtues, it did not include an address or
phone number anywhere in the ad for people to buy. You can bet
that megabucks were lost on that one.

Disciple Advocates Who Will Sell for You

George Chanos, creator of the board game Notable Quotables, had
no advertising budget the year his game made its national debut.
With a first run of 5,000 games, Chanos knew that he couldn't blow
any potential earnings on paid advertising. Plus, he simply didn't
have the budget. Almost all of the $465,000 he had raised from
investors had been socked into the design and printing of the game
and injection molding of the plastic game pieces.

Along with the media coverage he got as part of a public
relations campaign, Chanos relied on himself to spread the word

to anyone who would listen—from college classes to radio promotions directors. Chanos worked nonstop to create what he calls "Advocates"—people who believe in your product and advertise it for you—the ultimate word-of-mouth campaign.

The year before the game's debut, Chanos began wearing Notable Quotables golf and T-shirts everywhere he went, and the minute someone gave him a cue, he began talking about the game. "All someone had to do was say, 'Nice shirt,' or 'What's Notable Quotables?' and I'd start talking," says Chanos. "Whether it was an airline ticket agent or a clerk in the grocery store, I wanted as many people as possible to know about Notable Quotables and to have felt good that they met the game's inventor. I'd tell them how to play the game, the background of how I spent five years coming up with the quotes from celebrities, and why the game is so much fun. I liken my quest for advocates to a politician shaking hands at a factory in Des Moines. Even if a worker is a life-long Democrat, if he had never shaken Walter Mondale's hand but shook Ronald Reagan's, chances are he'd vote for Reagan. I want those who meet me to feel an affinity for my product so that when they see it in the store, or see another game advertised on television, they'll tell their friends and family about me and my game."

Chanos admits he wasn't above giving bribes to sway advocates in his direction. One lunch hour when he was buying a sandwich at a deli in the coastal community of Del Mar, California, Chanos realized how many people frequented the local gathering place each week. When he noticed that the four teenagers behind the counters were all wearing T-shirts with surfer or rock concert designs, he had an idea. He asked to speak to the owner, but when he learned that the owner wasn't there, he asked the kids if they'd be willing to wear the shirts every day if they had the opportunity to earn two dollars if they were wearing the T-shirt on the days he bought lunch there—approximately three times a week.

"The teens were perfect human billboards in position each day in a high- traffic area," says Chanos. "If all four of them wore the shirt during each of my three weekly visits, I would pay twenty-four dollars a week, and that's some of the cheapest advertising you can find!"

Several days after he made the offer, Chanos went back to see if the kids took him up on it and if the owner approved of the idea. He even offered to pay the owner a fee as compensation.

"If you want to sell your product or service, you must push forward at all times, and you must believe in yourself. If you don't, it will show; people will sense it, and they won't be comfortable believing in something that you don't."

When one radio news director received a news release on Notable Quotables, she admitted to being intrigued but weary of false messiahs. When Chanos learned of her skepticism, he called her and broke the ice by saying, "I'm George Chanos, and I understand you're a cynic. Well you know, you should be. Almost everyone with a new product will tell you that theirs is the hottest thing going and in most cases it isn't. I don't know if we do or not, but the reactions we're getting from the media, consumers, and toy stores lead us to believe that we do have something big."

After thirty minutes of conversation, during which Chanos extolled the virtues of his product, the news director was a confirmed Notable Quotables advocate and scheduled him as a guest on her talk show.

Talking about his game nonstop also led Chanos' company, Gamemakers, Ltd., to its next venture, a game called Praxis. "I let one of my old high school buddies know what I was doing one day, and he told me of someone else he knew who was inventing a game, and I ended up buying the rights to it," says Chanos.

The attorney turned game maker warns entrepreneurs that there is a fine line between being excited about your venture and overzealous. "It's hard for me not to cross that line, but if I come across as a fanatic, I test the boundaries of credibility," says Chanos. "I never say that our product is the best, but I do say that all indicators point that way. By maintaining some objectivity, you can rely on facts and evidence to support what you are saying—and win over even more advocates for your cause."

Don't Turn off the Engine
Just Because You're off the Ground

Even when you have loyal advocates working for you and ads pulling for you, advertising your business can't stop. When a young reporter asked William Wrigley during the heyday of his chewing gum empire why he continued to do so much advertising, the magnate responded, "Just because we're in the air doesn't mean we're going to shut off the engine."

But how do you know how much to invest in advertising? First, it must be large enough to achieve the desired objective, according to Augustino Turner who wrote "Cost-Effective Advertising" for the May 1989, *Small Business Reports*. Here are some of the guidelines that Turner set up.

1. **Historical method.** Based on projected sales, this method increases or decreases the previous year's budget by a given percentage or dollar amount.

2. **Fixed-sum method.** Determine how much to spend based on a certain amount for each product sold. If you allocated fifty cents for each unit, and you plan to sell 200,000, the ad budget would be $10,000.

3. **Percentage-of-sales method.** Allocate no less than 5 to 8 percent of projected sales when the product is a large-ticket item (profit margin of 25 to 50 percent). Allocate no less than 3 to 6 percent of sales for commercial or industrial products.

4. **Affordable method.** The ad budget equals the funds remaining after all other expenses are budgeted.

5. **Competitive method.** Firms using this tactic try to match or outspend their competitors.

6. **Profit margin method.** Multiply projected sales by the company's gross margin percentage. Multiply that by the average advertising-to-gross-profit ratio in the industry.

7. **Sales force-to-advertising method.** This is based on the cost of maintaining a sales force in relation to the amount of sales it generates. If the company spends $20,000 on a sales force to generate 80 percent of its business, it should be willing to

spend an additional $50,000 on advertising to generate 20 percent of sales.

Turner cautions businesses to realize these are parameters for setting a budget. They should be balanced with the desired results for the ad program.

Top Self-Marketing Secrets
Advertising Tricks and Tactics

1. Don't play the saturation game like the big guys do; use the sharpshooter approach and concentrate on those media with the highest concentration of your target audience.

2. Use advertising, not publicity, when you must control the message and timing.

3. If you have a service in which Yellow Pages and classified ads are appropriate, place the bulk of your advertising dollars there.

4. Your ad must convey that you are the best.

5. Hire freelancers who once worked for the big agencies to be on your creative team.

6. Use an outrageous offer to gain the foot traffic you need.

7. Write an advertorial—which uses the art of storytelling—to let readers see how your product can improve their lives.

8. Don't make customers work to get in touch with you.

9. Spread the word by discipling advocates who will sell your product for you.

10. Determine an advertising budget that is in balance with your desired results for the ad program.

14

A Plan for All Seasons
If You Don't Know Where You Are Going, You Might Not Get There

Why would we put a chapter on planning at the end of the book? We didn't want to lose you. Developing a plan to market and promote yourself or your business takes time, effort, and a dedication that most career climbers, new entrepreneurs, or busy, established businesses think they don't have. But without a map to guide you to your ultimate destination, treacherous roadblocks and time-consuming detours can keep you from reaching your goals. Try not to look at planning as an obligatory to do, but as a way to solve tangible problems like improving cash flow, generating new business, overcoming ill will, and meeting customer deadlines. Think of it as a way to solve problems before they arise. Be proactive. Don't leave your life or the success of your business to chance.

Bill Cantor, who heads the New York City executive search firm the Cantor Concern, advocates planning to his career seekers. "A good record and competence are tremendously important but will not guarantee your success," he says. "After you have decided what you want to do and are on your way to attaining those goals, you must make a conscious effort to improve and advance yourself. No one else can do it for you."

Planning doesn't stop once you open your business, close the deal, or earn the promotion. It's a constant process that demands concentration and hard work, but the payoff is worth it. By applying the planning techniques that sophisticated public relations and marketing professionals use to position their company, promote their cause, or sell their product, you can improve your business, advance your career, and improve every other facet of your life.

Get Away to Get Perspective

Nobody really *has* time to plan; you must *make* time for it. One of the best ways to plan for your business is to get away from the day-to-day routine and distractions. That means planning at home probably won't work either. Go to a quiet park, reserve a meeting room or a hotel suite, borrow a backyard with a pool from a neighbor, or rent a time-share cabin in the mountains.

Trish and Will Hunter, a husband-and-wife speaking team and authors of *Life Enrichment*, check themselves into a bayfront resort at the end of each fiscal year to review their performance and to plan for the ensuing year. They started this practice years ago when each of them was working for separate companies. Then, it was a time to look at how they had saved and spent their salaries and to evaluate their investments. Today, they not only look at their personal finances but also the finances of their joint speaking business.

Along with spreadsheets and bank statements, the Hunters bring another important piece of paper that they call their PACT (A Promise to Accept Commitment Together). It's a one- or two-sentence proclamation of a goal the two have agreed to previously. The Hunters began making PACTs more than twenty years ago, when they decided to marry. That first PACT read, "To work on it for as long as it was worth it."

"We wrote that commitment statement to one another on a tiny piece of paper, rolled it up tightly, tied it with a piece of Trish's hair, and stored it in her jewelry box," says Will. "It's our most valued possession."

Today, the Hunters have several new PACTs. When they embarked on their career as public speakers, the couple created a PACT that read, "We commit to becoming profitable and realizing the goals we have declared for our book and professional speaking career. This activity of financial, mental, physical, and spiritual resources will be the focus of our lives until April 1988, when we will evaluate our progress." On April 30, the Hunters unscrolled the PACT and realized that they had made enough progress to commit to another six months, and after that, another year.

"The most important piece of business we attend to at our annual planning retreat is to unscroll last year's PACT to see if we are on track and to determine if we are still willing to commit to the spirit of it," says Trish. "The PACT gives us perspective by letting us see how far we've come. It also helps us to refocus on the intent of our work and spurs us on to greater heights. Throughout the year when we're caught up in traveling to speak and deadlines for writing books and producing tape albums, we remember our PACT and we find new reason and motivation to keep moving forward. With a PACT, you are willing to commit to go beyond your fear and self-doubt."

Eight years ago, the Hunters also began mid-year evaluations as well. "During the year, we become involved in so many things that this serves as a moment of recommitment," says Will. "We make the evaluation fun, by going out of town if we can and really making it a time to congratulate ourselves for our progress. And it seems that the week after our evaluation, things immediately begin to happen! A PACT is a higher thought than a goal; it's a broad-based commitment."

As partners in life and business, Trish and Will are fortunate to have each other to share dreams. Don't try to plan alone. You need the synergy that comes from brainstorming sessions with others who care about your success. Ask your spouse, business partner, or key managers to join you in a planning session. Or invite your advisory board members, friends, or colleagues who have invested money in your venture.

"The idea behind planning is to clarify objectives for yourself, and it obviously involves others who have to buy into the plan, and need to see the big picture," says Fred Pryor, CEO of Pryor Resources, Inc., in Kansas City, Missouri, and founder of Fred Pryor Seminars. "When you plan with others, you will be able to get perspective on important issues that were in your blind spot. They serve as objective consultants who will force you to answer tough questions about what you have in mind.

They can help you determine if your thinking is clear and scrutinize your plan of action."

Pryor says that no matter how long your plan—one year, five years, or ten years—it's essential to be flexible. "Long-range goals can be vague, but the closer they get—say within a year or two—the more refined they must be," says Pryor. "Investing too much time to design a plan for more than a few years away from the present moment isn't wise. Too much is subject to change. But being very specific about what you plan to do this month and in six months is essential."

By specific, Pryor even means including details such as seminars you plan to attend, books you want to read, and new degrees you want to pursue. "Allocating time to personal growth and development is essential," he says.

To get the planning juices flowing, get away from the day-to-day pressures. You'll be surprised how much more creative and impartial you can be when you are in a new environment and surrounded by people who have dedicated the day or weekend to focus on one thing. You'll also foster visionary ideas if you allow this time of planning to be one in which people have fun and feel comfortable—both in dress and communication. Let your planning group know that this is a no-holds-barred time, during which they can speak freely about the direction of the company and its future.

As the leader of the pack, come prepared with some tools that will spur free thinking. Bring a flip chart, easel and colored pens, or an overhead projector, transparencies, and felt-tip markers. Write down your goals and the specific ideas that your planning group comes up with to help you meet them. Appoint a secretary to record ideas to take back to the office. If you have access to a portable computer, keyboarding input makes for easy reading when you return to the office and saves the time of transcription.

Any other background material you can bring to prime the pump of creative juices will help you get started. These might include

■ year-to-date sales
■ cash flow projections

- staffing structure
- a list of the product line
- samples, prototypes, photos, or a video tape of the product
- written description of your service
- marketing materials, such as brochures and direct mail letters
- advertisements placed
- media coverage to date, whether newspaper clippings or audio or video cassettes
- research about the competition, such as articles from trade journals
- results of name or copyright searches
- customer letters (satisfied and dissatisfied)
- customer service and return policies

Assemble an Advisory Board or Board of Directors

Many small businesses don't have the luxury of having shareholders who meet on a quarterly basis to help direct the business. But you can take your lead from nonprofit organizations that assemble voluntary boards of directors from interested community members who find satisfaction in giving back to the community and networking among peers.

Catherine Gauthier-Smith, owner of Intellisearch, a strategic management consulting firm, has put together a small board of directors to help guide her key business decisions. Two longtime business colleagues—the chairman of a bank and the chief financial officer of a Los Angeles corporation—who know and trust Catherine give their time to help her succeed.

"There are two main reasons I have a board of directors—one is legal and one is practical," Catherine explains. "Since Intellisearch is a corporation, I must have a board of directors that meets regularly. If I operate without a board, I risk losing the advantages of a corporation, which serves to shield me from the liabilities of the company. If someone were to sue, they would sue the corporation, and it would be more difficult to obtain a judgment against me personally."

"More importantly, my board doesn't just rubber-stamp my decisions. They take an active role in asking me why I am hiring, increasing my overhead, or going into debt. Recently when I sought to increase a line of credit to finance growing receivables, the board asked to see my financial analysis showing how it would be repaid. Presenting projections to such seasoned executives kept me from going headlong into debt without serious consideration. I knew what I was getting into and how I would get out. My board members take their responsibilities very seriously."

Finding individuals to become board of director members isn't always easy, since they hold a certain amount of liability for corporate action. Another alternative is to assemble an advisory board where the only thing at stake is friendship.

Members can be relatives, friends, and colleagues who have helped formulate your ideas; mentors who have offered advice over the years; other noncompeting business owners that you admire; bankers and other investors who have loaned you money; and even media contacts you have made. While, as a small business owner, you can't afford to pay these individuals, you can provide them with an opportunity to meet other key people in the community, to add an advisory board position to their résumé, and to learn new business pointers from others. Plus, you can return the favor by offering to serve in their company or community organization in some way.

So as not to take advantage of their generosity, hold no more than four advisory board meetings a year. Serve a meal, have a written agenda, and be open to any comments you get—even those you don't want to hear. Follow up after each meeting with thank you notes or telephone calls to express your appreciation. And always ask how you can assist them.

Throughout the year, keep the advisory board apprised of your major business moves. Send them copies of pertinent reports, sales figures, new product introductions, and media coverage. But don't inundate them. Make this material easy for them to file by giving them a three-ring binder with your company's name on it and sending material that has been three-hole drilled. Or send the material in file folders with the indexing tab already written for them.

Jack Berkman, Chairman and Chief Executive Officer of Berkman & Daniels, a marketing and communications firm, says he and his partner, Dick Daniels, formed an advisory board that includes a banker, an accountant, a major real estate executive, an attorney, and an entrepreneur who is chairman of an important business in the city. We meet with our advisory board quarterly to discuss our business' growth. These individuals are all visionaries, and they are ambassadors for our company.

In addition, Berkman & Daniels keeps other key people apprised of their company's message. "We have friends and clients who are VIPs, movers and shakers, presidents and chairmen of the board of important businesses and organizations to whom we send our corporate brochure press kit, and whom we update with news clippings about the job we are doing on a periodic basis. Making friends with people in key positions in business, politics, cultural, and community organizations is a business basic that has been instrumental in Berkman and Daniels' success. Of course, it starts with doing an excellent job that earns the leads and results in valuable third-party endorsements," says Berkman.

Plan with Your Key Audiences in Mind

Every step you take toward fulfilling your marketing plan is calculated with your customers or clients in mind. To make your planning precise, identify the various people on whom the success of your business depends. These people make up subsets called "publics." Here are a number of publics that a business might be trying to please.

- advisory board or board of directors
- potential customers or clients (who can also be divided into more precise subsets by age, occupation, interests and/or income level)
- current clients
- the community

- vendors
- colleagues
- constituents

Don't try to lump all of your various audiences into one amorphous "public." That's how amateurs plan. Remember, each subset has specific needs and desires. What is affecting one may not be a concern to another. Your marketing plan will include a variety of action strategies geared to these specific groups.

The Building Blocks of a Written Plan

As with all goals, you'll have a better chance of fulfilling your marketing goals if you commit them to paper. Don't just think great thoughts or espouse lofty goals. Be willing to put them in black and white and sign in blood. Getting this type of information down in writing forces you to think through some pretty tough questions about your career path or business. It will help you evaluate not only where you are going, but where you are and what it will take to claim that prized brass ring.

The following are essential elements the pros use in developing marketing and public relations plans. Adapt them for your own purposes. We credit the Public Relations Society of America and Professors Glen Broom, Ph.D., and David Dozier, Ph.D., of the Journalism Department at San Diego State University for their guidance in helping us understand the planning concept. Their pure public relations planning guides have been adapted here for the needs of our target public—readers of *Self-Marketing Secrets.* We trust, however, that though simplified, the spirit of the intent is not lost.

The public relations/marketing plan we suggest uses a goal/objective/action strategy format. Once you get the hang of it, it will help tremendously to plan for and monitor your business' success. We've outlined the steps below and included a sample plan at the end of this chapter.

1. Problem (or Opportunity) Statement. Remember we said that marketing and public relations solves problems. Your plan should begin by outlining problems or opportunities with your significant publics, such as employees, investors, and the media. Write this statement in the present tense so that it is active and dynamic, and describe your current situation in specific and measurable terms. Don't make judgments or place blame. Be as neutral as possible. And don't try to imply a solution—that comes later. The problem statement should be one paragraph of several sentences that answer the following questions:

■ What is the source of concern or the opportunity? (a brand new business, the need to attract new clients, a tainted image, quality of work that has suffered, a great product but only a limited number of people in a specific geographical area know about it, a lack of name recognition).

■ Where is this a problem? (in your city, throughout the country).

■ When is it a problem? (at the first of the year, around the holidays, whenever we introduce a new product).

■ Who is involved or affected? (clients, customers, employees, vendors).

Here are a few sample problem statements.

Problem 1: The ABC Company is a new weight-management program for executives that concentrates on learning how to eat in the real world. That emphasis needs to be communicated to executives in a way that differentiates the program from other diet programs, such as Nutri-System, Jenny Craig, Weight Watchers, and the Diet Center. Ten to fifteen clients per month are needed for the first three months to meet overhead and expenses.

Problem 2: DGF Educational Seminars is working to attract busy professionals—doctors, accountants, insurance agents—to its seminars and must create a need that will make these individuals take time out of their schedules to attend. Current seminars are attracting fifty to seventy-five people; eighty to one hundred are desired to generate the necessary profit margin.

Problem 3: Only 10 percent of the XYZ restaurant's business is return customers, resulting in a continual need to spend marketing and public relations dollars to attract tourists and new clientele. The restaurant must increase customer satisfaction to result in a 30 percent customer return rate over six months (a 20 percent increase).

Problem 4:   The budget is $20,000 short of the amount needed to launch the new product at the scheduled kickoff event on June 1. Key investors need to be attracted to the project.

Problem statements are more meaningful and useful when they contain concrete measurements of the problem, such as the number of customers or clients needed, the percent of increased business needed, or the amount of money needed. Speak in quantifiable terms, not gross generalities, such as "More business or capital is needed."

2. Situation Analysis. While the problem statement gives a concise description of the situation, the situation analysis is a summary of all that is known about your company's situation, the forces operating on it, and those publics involved or affected by it. It contains all of the background information that has brought your company to where it is today.

This part of your marketing/public relations plan illustrates, in detail, the meaning of the problem statement. Through analysis of the situation, you are able to clearly and specifically define and refine the problem statement.

The situation analysis includes a thorough summary of the perceptions and actions of key individuals and a history of your business. It might also include an overview of your communications to all of your publics. This helps to identify policies, procedures, and activities that impact your business and its bottom line.

It also provides information on events and conditions outside of your company, such as the competition and the economy. State how each of your audiences is involved or affected by these conditions. You must know what each group thinks and wants in order to set meaningful objectives and develop action strategies. Put simply, the situation analysis, takes off the blinders and helps you see what should be seen.

All this means that you probably need to conduct some research before you begin outlining ways to meet your objectives. Do you know who your existing and potential clients/customers are? Have you asked them to fill out brief surveys to find out who is buying your product/service? What are their ages, income levels, interests? Where do they live, work, and play? Why do they buy your product/service? How do they feel about issues that impact your business? How do they get their information? What are their opinions about the product/service you are planning to provide?

Don't assume or second guess. Too many people waste marketing dollars by guessing rather than asking what their publics want.

With specific information in hand, you can set objectives for each public and develop strategies to achieve them. Take time to analyze the marketplace so that you can set realistic goals. Avoid overpromising and underdelivering.

Writing a situation analysis helps to determine your position in the marketplace and gives you a benchmark from which to work. Even if you don't review your situation analysis until six months or a year later, when you update your marketing plan, you will be able to compare where you are now to where you were. Seeing how much you've accomplished is reward enough for writing it.

Here is an abbreviated situation analysis for an employee-assistance company that provides counseling services to a company's employees for such things as substance abuse, marital or family problems, legal problems, or illnesses.

LMN Company, an employee-assistance company in Anytown, offers a variety of services beyond the traditional employee-assistance program benefits, including: six monthly visits per employee (most offer three); legal, financial, and health insurance assistance; and a twenty-four-hour help line. The services are offered at a lower price than the competition. In addition, LMN Company offers management training and post-traumatic counseling. LMN also will tailor services to meet the needs of a contracting firm.

Sue Jones purchased LMN Company and took over the accounts of twelve existing clients. In two years, the company attracted six new accounts. It wanted to add two new accounts per month over the next six months.

Competition for the corporate employee benefit dollar has increased. That, combined with the sharp increase in the cost of health insurance, has caused a decrease in the amount of money an employer is willing to spend on ancillary health-related services. Current competition includes 123 firms and 567 consultants. Research, in the form of a questionnaire sent to 100 companies, indicated that LMN Company had name recognition among human resource decision makers. Sixty-two percent had heard of the company, twenty-one percent had not, and seventeen percent could not remember. Monthly contract costs and the number of visits per employee per year were the two primary considerations human resource directors use when selecting an employee-assistance firm.

3. Opportunities and Threats. State, in laundry-list form, what is working in your favor and what is not. What has made this an opportune time or situation for you to start, expand, or aggressively market your specific business? What impending danger looms out there that you need to recognize? Making a list of these types of pros and cons forces you to take a hard look at the opportunities you face and the obstacles you must overcome.

Identify whether your product/service is unique, how it differs from others, and what kind of need or desire your business meets. Outline the type of competition you face and any guilt-by-association you must overcome. Is the market saturated? Has something been reported in the media that will make this a particularly good or bad time to launch or promote your business or product/service?

The following are some threats and opportunities faced by Dr. X, a plastic surgeon opening a new office in a new city:

Threats

- Five other plastic surgeons have established practices in the same medical office park as Dr. X.

- It takes time to build personal relationships and gain referrals from other physician specialists.
- Questionable advertising techniques by some cosmetic surgeons have made many consumers leery of promotional campaigns conducted by physicians.

Opportunities

- Dr. X has superb educational and private practice credentials.
- Dr. X is a plastic surgeon with strengths in reconstructive, microsurgery, and cosmetic surgery and will be able to build his practice with a varied patient load.
- Studies show that increasing numbers of business people, both men and women, are seeking cosmetic surgery in order to advance in their careers; so the patient base for this medical specialty is increasing.

4. Goals. The goals are the most important statement in the marketing and/or public relations plan. They outline what you hope to accomplish over a specific time period. Goals are the payoff and must also be stated in specific terms of what will be achieved. Make them doable, not too modest or too ambitious. State not only what you plan to achieve but also by what specific date. Be sure the outcome can be measured.

Goal statements generally involve the change or maintenance of behavior of your target publics. A good goal statement includes

- Your target audience(s).
- The desired behavior.
- The amount of change you desire, stated in quantifiable terms, such as percentages.
- The time frame in which you estimate the goal can reasonably be achieved.
- The geographical area where all of this will take place.

Below are a few sample goal statements.

1. Increase the number of diamond ring sales during the winter and spring months (before summer weddings) from ten to fifteen per month at the center city mall outlet.

2. Increase the number of four-color printing jobs in the new shop by 15 percent between January 1 and June 30.
3. Establish a client base of twenty biweekly customers at the Nail Emporium by January 1.
4. Obtain five new business leads a month that will generate $100,000 monthly insurance sales by December 31 in the metropolitan area.

5. Publics. Your plan generally focuses on one or more publics. Here you precisely define each public. Who are these people? How is this public characterized? What are its demographics and psychographics—including age, sex, lifestyle, media usage, and political affiliation? What is the relationship between the public and the organization/program? Why is the public's relationship with the business important? How is that public involved in the business/program?

Publics for an accounting firm would include the following:

■ Small businesses without in-house accounting.

■ Private citizens interested in tax planning and filing services.

■ Bankers and financial planners who serve as potential referral sources.

■ Current clients.

6. Objectives. Now, break each goal down into measurable objectives by your publics in order of importance. Include a time frame, as you did in the goal statement.

Just as goals define the overall outcome for the entire marketing/public relations program, objectives state desired outcomes for each of your publics. You should have a goal statement for each defined public, and each public may have two or more objectives. By reaching the objectives for each group, the overall goals of the program are achieved.

Here is an example of a goal and objective in the public relations/marketing plan for *Notable Quotables*, a trivia-based board game that made its debut during the holiday season.

To sell 5,000 games locally as a test market for the game during the holiday season. To use these results as a way to entice toy buyers at the annual International Toy Fair.

To entice 120 local toy store owners to purchase the game and display it in their stores during November and December.

7. Action Strategies. At last you're ready for action. List all of the possible moves you must make to achieve each objective, thereby meeting the goal. Unfortunately, this is where many people start their planning. But you really can't determine the action until you have conducted initial research, identified the problem, analyzed the situation, and determined quantifiable goals and objectives.

This is where you designate the specific steps you will take to meet each objective, such as local, national, or trade journal media relations; speaker's bureau campaign; or direct mail campaign. You will also identify what you will have to produce—news releases, brochures, flyers, newsletters, direct mail pieces, etc.

Ask yourself: What information needs to be communicated to achieve the objective for each public? How does the information need to be tailored so that the specific public will understand it? What is the best medium in which to get the message out to the public?

This is also a time when you create a calendar of things to do; pencil out a corresponding budget; and assign activities to staff members, consultants, friends, relatives, and supporters.

Here are a few action strategies for a family business consultant intent on building her client base. These action strategies appeared under various objectives for particular publics (as demonstrated in the sample marketing/public relations plan that follows this chapter).

1. Develop a brochure to explain services and list current clients. Include anecdotes of how the consultant has solved problems unique to family owned ventures.

2. Create a news release to be sent to business sections of daily newspapers and business newspapers identifying specific news angles.

3. Identify a feature angle for *Family Business* magazine, an industry trade journal.

4. Send the brochure with a cover letter that identifies the consultant as a speaker who tackles tough issues of concern to family owned business and professional organizations.

And the list goes on.

Don't Forget to Evaluate

The Achilles heel of many public relations/marketing programs is weak feedback about how well objectives and goals were met. Beware: Evaluation is not the number of brochures distributed, direct mail brochures sent, or column inches that result from a news release.

Evaluation means measuring how well the objectives were achieved for each activity, and the goal, overall. The smart self-marketer builds evaluation methods into the plan so that all the eggs are not in one basket if a specific action strategy flops.

Throughout the program, assess how things are going. As you get into the campaign, identify whether or not additional background information or insights would make you change directions. Instead of wishing that things could be different, make them different. Were any key publics missed? Did you make some assumptions that proved to be wrong? Did certain angles not attract the media as you thought? Did a crisis arise that you didn't anticipate?

Use hindsight to critically analyze your efforts and to help guide you to an even brighter future. That's why politicians use follow-up polls after debates on the campaign trail—and that's why they frequently change their tactics midway.

Here are some questions to ask yourself to help grade your efforts.

- Did the message communicated meet the needs and desires of the target publics?
- Were communications accurate and timely?
- Were there adverse reactions to messages or actions?

- Did corrective actions help or hinder?
- Were staff and budget adequate for the plan?

Time for an Attitude Adjustment

Once you've evaluated results, adjust your plan, taking into consideration both positive and negative evaluations. Use your evaluation to improve future programs. Identify the goals and objectives that will be the most difficult to achieve. What are the consequences of not achieving them? How might they be approached next time to improve chances of success? Explain how future programs might be modified to reduce negative consequences and undesired outcomes and to increase opportunities for meeting your goals in the next round.

Whether you are building a company or advancing in your career, don't leave anything to chance. Know what you want to do and why. Then as Nike says, "Just do it!"

Marketing/Public Relations Plan
prepared for
ABC Restaurants

EXECUTIVE SUMMARY

ABC Restaurant, a family owned and operated restaurant, was established in Anytown, USA, in 1976. The restaurant has created visibility and distinction for itself through its dramatic architecture and position on a busy downtown intersection.

An informal poll revealed that diners remembered enjoying meals at ABC Restaurant. But because the food does not fit into a specific category and the atmosphere within the restaurant lacks definition, patrons have no recollection of what they ate. Therefore, a specific image — good or bad — has not been attained.

The marketing plan for ABC Restaurant will create an image and a niche for the restaurant that will increase its utilization, and thus sales and profits, within the next quarter.

The restaurant customer mix in the past has been 60 percent new business and 40 percent repeat customers. It is not known how often the repeat customers return or how many of the first-time customers are tourists. However, lunch patrons are a more loyal crowd, and the restaurant is busy at lunchtime during the work week. Thus, this marketing plan will concentrate on increasing repeat business during the dinner hours.

The following plan outlines suggested activities for the next three months, focusing on image enhancement and media relations.

SITUATION ANALYSIS

Opportunities

- Sixty percent of the patrons are visiting the restaurant for the first time. They have no preconceived notions about the restaurant and provide opportunities for potential repeat business.

- The restaurant has been remodeled recently to offer a new, more appealing and more comfortable atmosphere.

- ABC Restaurant has a fashionable new "American/Pacific Rim" menu that stimulates diners' interest and offers many media angles.

- There is not a negative impression of the restaurant or its food to overcome.

- The owners of the restaurant are progressive and willing to try new approaches in order to meet the needs of their clients.

Threats

- Only forty percent of the patrons who visit the restaurant are compelled to return again.

- "American/Pacific Rim" food is new and not a proven success. It could be perceived as a quick fad such as "California Cuisine" or "Cajun Food."

- The service at ABC Restaurant has not always been rated as warm, quick, or friendly — all of which would be good reasons to return. In a recent survey, service was rated as the second most important quality in choosing a restaurant, signaling that ABC Restaurant would benefit greatly by attempting to improve its service.

- Competition has increased in the last decade. Consumers can select from a wide variety of foods and atmospheres for their dining experience. According to an XYZ survey, great seafood is the first choice of diners in the downtown area, followed by the atmosphere of waterfront restaurants, then Mexican food, and finally by Italian. ABC Restaurant does not fit into any of the top four categories. This could become a golden opportunity if maximized. While the increased savvy of Anytown diners has encouraged them to venture out more, the proliferation of restaurants has given them a wide choice among would-be suitors.

GOALS

Long-Term:

To create an image and mystique for the new ABC Restaurant that will intrigue Anytowners and make them eager to try this newest hot spot. To increase repeat business from the current 40 percent to 60 percent in the next six months. To have the service given by ABC Restaurant employees recognized as superb.

Short-Term (Three Months):

To increase awareness in downtown Anytown and surrounding areas of the new "American/Pacific Rim" restaurant image, comfortable interior

decor, and tantalizing "American/Pacific Rim"
menu. To research exactly what customers think
about ABC Restaurant and what they want from it,
then to adjust the restaurant accordingly. To get
people talking positively about ABC Restaurant.

Target Publics

- Anytowners between ages 30 and 50 who
  have some discretionary income for dining
  out and spend an average of $20 to $30 a
  meal.

- Business professionals working in the
  downtown area who are able to frequent
  ABC Restaurant for lunch.

- Tourists visiting Anytown and
  tourist-related industries such as
  hotels, motels, and travel agencies.

- Anytowners who are interested in happy
  hour and evening entertainment.

- The food-oriented elite who faithfully
  follow the newest food trends and pore
  over advice given by restaurant reviewers.

PROGRAM OBJECTIVES

Objective 1

Research current customer satisfaction, needs,
tastes, and wants to determine the best marketing
approach for increasing business.

Action Strategies

A. Put surveys, with five key questions about
service and food, on the tables. Offer a small

discount off their next meal as a thank you for taking the time to fill out the questionnaire.

This will give ABC Restaurant valuable information from its customers, as well as communicating that their input is so valuable you are willing to pay for it (via the discount on their next meal). The survey questions will change monthly or quarterly.

Tabulate and produce results of these surveys monthly.

B. Conduct a mall survey asking shoppers key questions pertinent to ABC Restaurant such as: "Have you ever been to ABC Restaurant?" "What did you think?" "Why not?" or "What would entice you to try the restaurant?" This information will help determine if there is a stigma attached to the restaurant, or it will explain why people aren't coming back. It will also serve as a benchmark from which marketing efforts can be measured.

Tabulate results and use to enhance marketing plan/efforts.

Objective 2

Increase customer satisfaction in the area of service.

Action Strategies

A. Through internal public relations, create a team spirit so employees are encouraged to provide better, more cheerful, and more accommodating service. Create incentives for pleasing the customers. Put time guarantees on how long it will take for each dish to reach the table.

B. Make games available for the customers while they are waiting for their food. For example,

Chinese checkers, word games, backgammon. These games will also serve to attract couples with children. (Most people in the target age range do have children.)

C. Create an inexpensive appetizer that can be placed on the table while people are waiting for their food. (Similar to tortilla chips and salsa at a Mexican restaurant.) If the appetizer is unique enough, people will crave it and come to the restaurant just for the appetizer. For example, Chinese fried noodles with a tangy peach or mustard sauce.

Develop promotional material to publicize the specials, such as "Frequent Flyers" distributed in the downtown area and mailed to the ABC Restaurant's existing mailing list and new names acquired through surveys and promotions.

Objective 3

Create a frenzy for American/Pacific Rim food and atmosphere in order to establish an image and niche for the new ABC Restaurant.

Action Strategies

A. Media Relations: The goal of the media relations campaign is to position the owners as the experts on Pacific Rim cuisine, and to position ABC Restaurant as the first name for Pacific Rim entrees. A telephone index card titled, for example, "Pacific Rim Cuisine Expert" will be sent to appropriate media. These cards will also be sent to local businesses and business groups who might be interested in dining at the restaurant.

Identify intriguing news angles about ABC Restaurant and American/Pacific Rim food, then send news releases and personalized queries to daily, weekly and monthly papers, magazines, trade journals, and producers of local radio and television programs. Some national magazines such as *In-Flights* and *Travel* will also be queried.

B. Have the decor of the restaurant cleverly show aspects of the American/Pacific Rim experience. For example, hang photos from the Pacific Rim with explanatory captions about lifestyles, customs, and local color. This will help diners identify with the American/Pacific Rim.

C. Conduct American/Pacific Rim Gourmet Cooking Clinics with the restaurant's star chef preparing American/Pacific Rim specialties that can be made at home. Unique spices could be available for purchase in ABC Restaurant packaging. An "American/Pacific Rim Cooking Video" could be a spin-off of successful cooking clinics. These videos would be available at the restaurant.

D. Place tent cards on the tables explaining to the customers exactly what the Pacific Rim is and how the food flavorings at ABC Restaurant fit into the American/Pacific Rim category.

E. Host luncheons for local business groups that hold monthly meetings during the noon hour. Feature a short presentation on the Pacific Rim and American/Pacific Rim dining.

Identify appropriate business groups, develop a publicity angle, and coordinate the program accordingly.

F. Host a month-long "Coming Out" celebration for the soft Grand Opening. During this month, feature lots of American/Pacific Rim dishes with tantalizing smells and colorful presentations during "Happy Hour" and offer an American/Pacific Rim appetizer sampler for half price on the menu.

Develop the party theme, publicize the ongoing event, and evaluate the success of the plan.

G. Give each dish on the menu a clever or scintillating name that ties into the American/Pacific Rim. Also, make the descriptions of the dishes witty, fun, and imaginative. This will help to reinforce the identity of the food.

Write, design, and produce a new menu for ABC Restaurant to complement the new vibrant image.

H. Feature festive American/Pacific Rim music and entertainment to help add to the American/Pacific Rim atmosphere.

I. Sell ABC Restaurant T-Shirts at the cash register. These can also be used as Radio Giveaways in conjunction with free dinners at ABC Restaurant. Design and produce the T-shirts to be sold at the restaurant and arrange promotions with local radio celebrities.

Objective 4

Create a desire in first-time customers to become regulars and to bring friends or to recommend the restaurant to others who might become loyal patrons of ABC Restaurant.

A. Newsletters — Current customers are more likely than cold prospects to return to ABC Restaurant and to refer your services to others in the target market. A bi-monthly or quarterly newsletter is one way to keep in touch with this important audience, to remind them of the terrific dining and entertainment you provide, and to give them valuable information that they can share with other prospects. It can also be used as a sales tool for mailing to new prospects.

Supplement the client-based mailing list to include your target market. A note on the tent card or questionnaire will ask diners if they want to be added to the mailing list.

B. Start a "Recipe of the Month" club. Each month a specific recipe will be available on a laminated card <u>at the restaurant only</u>. The recipe is only available during its featured month. Recipe card boxes could be sold at the restaurant. A table-top card could ask, "Do you like our food? Ask for our free recipes."

C. Publicize that private parties are held at ABC Restaurant. The Pacific Rim frenzy will be the theme. Catering for off-site events and parties could be a spin-off of this idea.

Identify the appropriate markets that would be interested in private party information, create collateral material to be sent to this audience, and coordinate follow-up accordingly.

# # #

Top Self-Marketing Secrets

A Plan for all Seasons

1. Make time to plan and do so away from your daily routine.

2. Create an advisory board or board of directors to gain key insights and perspective.

3. Put your plan in writing using the following format: goal/objective/strategy.

Recommended Readings

School is never out for the professional. Nor is it over for the self-marketer. Below are several books we recommend to help you make your name known.

Big Marketing Ideas for Small Service Businesses by Marilyn and Tom Ross (Dow-Jones-Irwin, 1990) concentrates on helping service industry professionals—lawyers, doctors, financial advisors and consultants—market their practices. It includes samples of sales letters, direct mail campaigns, and advertising for several different service markets.

Expose Yourself by Melba Beals (Chronicle Books, 1990) explains how to use the power of public relations to promote your business and yourself. The author is a former NBC television news reporter turned publicist.

Personal Marketing Strategies by Mike McCaffrey with Jerry Derloshon (Prentice-Hall, 1983) covers how to sell yourself, your ideas, and your services.

Street Smart Marketing by Jeff Slutsky (John Wiley & Sons, 1989) presents information on cross-promotions, neighborhood networking, free local publicity, community promotional techniques, and tele-selling. It offers sales-generating techniques such as getting businesses and organizations to distribute advertising for free, negotiating media buying deals without hiring a professional, and structuring promotions so that they are newsworthy.

The Secrets of Practical Marketing for Small Business by Herman R. Holtz (Prentice-Hall, 1986) focuses on marketing techniques for the small entrepreneur. It defines marketing, tells how to research, write, and implement a marketing plan. Specifics are given on writing advertisements and news releases.

The Young & Rubicam Traveling Creative Workshop by Hanley Horins (Prentice-Hall, 1990) distills 65 years of experience by one of the nation's greatest advertising and public relations agencies.

Self-Marketing Secrets Index